ONCE UPON A DREAM

Shropshire & Staffordshire

Edited By Elle Berry

First published in Great Britain in 2019 by:

Young Writers Est. 1991

Young Writers
Remus House
Coltsfoot Drive
Peterborough
PE2 9BF
Telephone: 01733 890066
Website: www.youngwriters.co.uk

FOREWORD

Welcome Reader, to a world of dreams.

For Young Writers' latest competition, we asked our writers to dig deep into their imagination and create a poem that paints a picture of what they dream of, whether it's a make-believe world full of wonder or their aspirations for the future.

The result is this collection of fantastic poetic verse that covers a whole host of different topics. Let your mind fly away with the fairies to explore the sweet joy of candy lands, join in with a game of fantasy football, or you may even catch a glimpse of a unicorn or another mythical creature. Beware though, because even dreamland has dark corners, so you may turn a page and walk into a nightmare!

Whereas the majority of our writers chose to stick to a free verse style, others gave themselves the challenge of other techniques such as acrostics and rhyming couplets. We also gave the writers the option to compose their ideas in a story, so watch out for those narrative pieces too!

Each piece in this collection shows the writers' dedication and imagination – we truly believe that seeing their work in print gives them a well-deserved boost of pride, and inspires them to keep writing, so we hope to see more of their work in the future!

CONTENTS

Kia Louise Roberts (11)	62
Poppy Asterley (9)	63
Phoebe Olivia Jervis (11)	64
Thomas Marsh (11)	65
Nathan Derrick Colin Woodhouse (11)	66
Matthew Harry Lloyd (11)	67
Emily Erin Moreton (11)	68
Jaydn Gary Phillip James Peart (10)	69
Cameron Philip Cotton (11)	70
Jolie Amber Lily Phillips (11)	71
Layla Evans (9)	72
Charlie Farmer (11)	73

Hazel Slade Primary Academy, Hazel Slade

Maddison Ford (10)	74
Hollie Rachel Eileen Timms (10)	75
Ezra Nathaniel Davies (8)	76
Vinny Coxon (10)	77
Amelia Harrison (10)	78
Matthew Peakman (10)	79
Caitlan Haywood (9)	80
Daniel Tonks (10)	81

Hollinswood Primary School, Hollinswood

Hollie Hunter (10)	82
Phoebe Willis (10)	84
Kamilya Sharif (9)	85
Daisy Louise Morris (10)	86
Brooke Marie Benevento (10)	87
Eesa Faisal (10)	88
Holly Reed (9)	89
Evrim Randa (10)	90
Jake Weston (10)	91
Mia Crofts (10)	92
Kane Young (10)	93
Nadusha Iyne (10)	94
Tia Biram (10)	95
Conrad Babane (10)	96

Ciara Priede-Wilson (9)	97
Buddy Powell (9)	98
Alfie Raymond Ferguson (9)	99
Jeenna-Faith Trueman (10)	100
Marcel Starszewski (9)	101

John Wilkinson Primary School, Broseley

George Halstead (10)	102
Joshua Lowe (10)	104
Ethan Arch (10)	106
Darcey Phillips (10)	107
Hollie Parfitt (10)	108
Louisa Mary Evans (10)	109
Joe Phillips (10)	110
Elijah Beau Campbell (9)	111
Joseph Elcock Price Jones (10)	112
Harry John Littlewood (9)	114
Max Illingworth (10)	115
Ellena Hemmings (10)	116
Luca Piotr Candlin (10)	117
Isla Gibb (10)	118
Euan Meek (9)	119
Travis Meek (9)	120
Mollie Eliza Hall (10)	121
Samuel McCreadie (10)	122
Holly Lewis-Dowell (10)	123
Kira Jones (10)	124
Ethan Worthington (10)	125
Amelia Burgess (10)	126
Jude Baxter (10)	127
William Satchwell (10)	128

St Mary's Catholic Primary School, Madeley

Angelo Rafael Leuterio Damalerio (8)	129
Summer Lucy Grace Jones (8)	130
Evelyn O'Sullivan (9)	132
Laura Jane Lewis (9)	133
Ami-Lee Mary Roseblade (9)	134
Olivia Holt (11)	135

Peyton Farmer (9)	136	Leya Jacob (7)	173
Poppy Lowndes (7)	137	Daniella Hathaway (10)	174
Amy Thomas (9)	138	Oscar Lomas (9)	175
Bindiya Aujla (8)	139	Megan Hovers (10)	176
Bethany Thomas (10)	140	Ava Mae Cruise (8)	177
Fearne Scarlett Rose Finnigan (10)	141	Edward Fletcher-McCraight (10)	178
River Ann Jones (9)	142	Connie Costelloe (9)	179
Fabian Ciornei (10)	143	Ben Jacob (10)	180
Amelia Rose Havard (8)	144	Samuel Benstead (9)	181
Davina Mann (7)	145	Alexis Mabatid (10)	182
Izabella Thomas (7)	146	Anna James (10)	184
Luca Eitel Fotso (8)	147	Annmiya Tharappel (10)	185
Wilma-Thelma Sam (9)	148	Jerusha James (9)	186
Taylor-May Skyvington (8)	149	Michalina Dytrych (10)	187
Zsa-Zsa Rowland (8)	150	Benjamin Aaron Paredes Amigo (9)	188
Kacy-Leigh Kniveton (7)	151		
Ethan Humphries (8)	152	Marc Antony Howells (10)	189
Teigan Skyvington (10)	153	Elena Charalambous (10)	190
Elisha Pledger (7)	154	Daniel Kolodziej (9)	191
Vladut Cristian Popa (8)	155	Leon Jacob	192
Jessica Griffiths (7)	156	Abel Tharappel (7)	193
Jordan Van Jaarsveld (10)	157	Agata Maria Ignatiuk (9)	194
Meghan Canty (8)	158	Ania Maria Kunicka (10)	195
Zuzanna Milczarek (10)	159	Isaac Kiley (9)	196
Imogen Groom (8)	160	Gaspar Zajdlewicz (10)	197
Joshua Hughes (8)	161	Dillon Moore (10)	198
Benos Juskevicius (8)	162	Monika Olechowska (9)	199
Lena Sulkowska (9)	163	Martyna Anna Denis (10)	200
Isabelle Maddison White (8)	164	Seb H (10)	201
		Libby Clarke (8)	202
		Angelina Sebastian (9)	203

St Matthew's CE (A) Primary School, Donnington

Joshua George Walton (9)	165

Blanka Zajdlewicz (8)	204
Jared Pestano (10)	205
Oliver Senior (9)	206

St Modwen's Catholic Primary School, Burton-On-Trent

Lilly Hovers (8)	166
Maksymilian Zimnoch (10)	168
Jayami Dinara Hewawasan Ranaweerage (9)	170
Nikola Zuralska (10)	172

Stoke Minster CE Primary Academy, Stoke-On-Trent

Summer Ratcliffe (9)	207
Olivia Grace Steele (10)	208
Ayaan Hussain (10)	209
Ryan Davies (10)	210
Abirsana Gnanavadivel (9)	211
Ali Shah (10)	212

THE POEMS

The Heaven With Unicorns!

Hi Ms Unicorn!
Last night I could see unicorns in my dream
So in the middle of the night
I woke up because I felt really thirsty and my throat
was dry.
But then at that moment
I spotted something in the window
I froze on the spot
I courageously stepped out of my bedroom...
Just then I stepped out
I couldn't believe it
I was in Heaven!
I saw a unicorn
It was you, Ms Unicorn!
I could see your colourful wings spreading out
And I could see your spiky hair
These were stars illuminating on the horizon like
lanterns
These were fireflies creating a majestic rainbow.
Ms Unicorn, if you don't mind
Take me away from here and take me to Heaven to the
place you like.
I hope you arrive soon where my destination is.

Aisha Parveen (10)
Anglesey Primary Academy, Burton-On-Trent

The Magical Dream Doors

Today I had an unusual nightmare,
I heard a mouse under my bed
And tried to catch it but I failed.
I tiptoed after it and then I opened the magical door...
I trudged and trudged and trudged through the blue,
soft portal.
I was surprised because the house looked like mine,
But a little bit interesting to be honest.

I smelt some dinner in the kitchen
But I was afraid to go there,
Slowly I walked into the room.
I saw Mum cooking some salad and chicken,
When she turned around she had b... b... b... buttons!

So I bolted so fast that I could hardly breathe,
The black, dull cat came with Whibie (my friend) to
save me.
Now we were ready for the war...

Vanessa Nicola Pisarkiewicz (10)
Anglesey Primary Academy, Burton-On-Trent

Planet Roll Call

Eight planets around the sun,
Listen as I call each one;
Mercury? Here! Number one, closest planet to the sun.
Venus? Here! Number two, shining bright, just like new!
Earth? Here! Number three! Is home to you and me.
Mars? Here! Number four! Red and ready to explore.
Jupiter! Here! Number five. The largest planet that's not a jive.
Saturn? Here! Number six! With rings of dust and ice that mix.
Uranus? Here! Number seven! A planet tilted high in Heaven!
Neptune? Here! Number eight, with one dark spot whose fire is great!

Sorana Criveanu (10)

Anglesey Primary Academy, Burton-On-Trent

My Mermaid World

I jumped in the ocean
With all kind of emotions
I couldn't believe what I could see
A whole new world before me.

My legs turned into a shiny tail
I could not believe what was about to unveil
It was a dream come true
Like a picture I once drew.

I met the underwater king and queen
They were something I had never seen
The king and queen were very sweet
They give me a talking coral to keep.

Then I saw my friends on the shore
I really wanted to see them more
I waved goodbye to my mermaid friend
I wish this did not have to end.

Zara Perveen (10)
Anglesey Primary Academy, Burton-On-Trent

Easter Island

The children on Easter Island,
Are really, really lucky,
The island was so big,
The children saw the Easter Bunny,
Named Bucky.

The animals were energetic,
Playing round in the sun,
Either playing or relaxing,
They all went to collect,
Baby Easter Bunny

The king was there,
Relaxing in the sun,
Chocolate dripped like lava,
The children found,
The egg bunny.

The Easter Bunny
Took us all on a VIP trip,
We all had lots of fun,
We all held on tight with lots of grip.

Billy Head (9)
Anglesey Primary Academy, Burton-On-Trent

Rhyme

Let's talk in rhyme all day
You know I hate to talk that way
Why not? It's lots of fun
Rhyming is fit for everyone
Oh, alright I'll have a go
But don't expect me just to know
Rhyming words from my head
I'd rather eat or lie in bed
Hey, I was rhyming too!
It's so much fun to do
But now I think it's time to go
And I'd really like you just to know
That you can rhyme as well as me
And so can they and he or she.

Ellis Laity (10)
Anglesey Primary Academy, Burton-On-Trent

Mr Dino!

I close my eyes and I can see a world made for me,
A dino as big as the entire universe,
I take a step forward, as nervous as I can be.
For it's a giant stegosaurus I see,
I fear the giant beast, so black
But suddenly, I'm on his scaly back,
I'm laughing as I look around
As my body goes up and down,
Stomp, stomp, stomp!
A dino named Topsy,
Make me and my sister so happy,
My sister was scared no more,
That's for sure.

Reem Cheema (9)
Anglesey Primary Academy, Burton-On-Trent

Back In Time

Back in time,
Doing just fine,
Stegosaurus, raptors,
All are dinosaurs,
Living back in time,
See the flowers dance,
Like a ballerina,
Hear water splashing around us,
Not that big of a fuss,
All living in a bush
I don't want them to mush me,
They have fleas.

Ryan Lee Rushton (9)
Anglesey Primary Academy, Burton-On-Trent

The Dream Wolf

Can you remember when the wolf sang?
Shouted, twirling, and flipping?
Her eyes as dark as space
You could hear the music ring,
No matter where you were!
You could see the wolf dance!
They can howl in the moonlight!
Best pets ever!

Nicole Piatek (9)
Anglesey Primary Academy, Burton-On-Trent

Furious Dancers

Let's get the dancer in a line,
Spinning, whirring, jumping, whirling around,
Determined eyes to win the candy house,
My unicorn friend ate the candy house,
Angry red faces glaring at the unicorn
Like a frustrated sun.

Saliha Waseem (9)
Anglesey Primary Academy, Burton-On-Trent

Monster Land

There was a boy called Tom,
He dreamt about a house made out of chocolate.
Tom ate like a tiger
But just then a monster came
The monster was friendly
But the killer clown was not...

Elitsa Kasapova (8)
Anglesey Primary Academy, Burton-On-Trent

Magic Dreams

The little, bright star twinkles in the night,
The puppy in the candyfloss house
Spins fast like a ballerina,
The famous dancer does athletics,
Then they dance all night long.

Tyesha-Destiny Cavanagh (9)
Anglesey Primary Academy, Burton-On-Trent

Enderman King

I woke up to a Minecraft world
Owned by King Fred Enderman
Then sizzling happened.
Bang! An explosion
Was like a rocket exploding.
A wither blew up the End bricks down.
There were boulders that broke the gated towers
down.
The boulders were stealing the walls down.
King Fred had another
And forth came the wither
Creeper pigs came and tried to blow up the wither.
Then Fred punched wither
And sent him back where he came from
And I woke up from a strange dream.

Leo Matthew Carins (12)
Cicely Haughton School, Wetley Rocks

The Most Extreme Packs

I woke up and opened FIFA packs.
Then packed ninety-nine, Pelé, and ninety-eight,
Maradona.
Then I had some pop.
Then it went *Fizz! Fizz! Fizz!*
Then I was like, "OMG!"
Because I packed Pelé and then I was flipping!
Then I packed everyone.

Jay Cunningham (9)
Cicely Haughton School, Wetley Rocks

Let's See Things In Candy Land

It's another morning in Candy Land,
Let's go see the marshmallows who are very tanned,
Let's see the gumdrops who think that candy is called
'cand',
Let's see the Skittles who love to be found.

Let's see the Fruit Pastllles that live in the shade,
Let's see the Starburst that like cherryade,
Let's see the Mentos that like to eat,
Let's see the lollipops that have a pool that they made.

Let's see the sugar that is very sweet,
Let's see the Maoams that like to eat,
Let's see the jelly snakes that have no feet,
Let's see the Polos that hate wheat,

Let's see the Sour Patch that does not like being fake,
Let's see the Toxic Waste that always aches,
Let's see the Haribos that like going to the lake
Let's see the gummy bears that like being awake.

Leah Walker (9)
Edge Hill Junior School, Stapenhill

The Mouse Monster

There was a lovely friend called Penny,
Who had a nice boyfriend called Kenny,
There was another friend called Jess,
Who's hair was always in a mess,
Last but not least,
There was a girl called Florence,
Floss for short.
Whose dad had to sort,
Lots of cool, amazing stuff,
Which was strong and tough,
Anyway, the three friends went to Jess' house,
Where Jess had a white pet mouse,
Suddenly, the mouse looked up,
While it was swelling to the size of a tall cup,
Eventually, it turned into a monster size,
Then Floss said, "This is nonsense and lies."
The mouse monster looked and grabbed Floss,
Because it was very cross,
The mouse monster lazily went outside,
So did the other three,
Strangely, Penny looked like she was thinking
Floss would be squashed like a pea,
Quickly, Penny and Jess got something,
Which looked like wings

Penny attached the wings on Jess' arms,
Wrapping the ends around her wrists like a bracelet with charms,
Then Jess started to frantically flap her wings,
To fly up and save Floss before anyone could say, "Ping!"
Jess flapped and flapped
While she rapped and rapped
Until the mouse monster let go of Florence from all the breeze
Then Jess caught Floss who was eating some yellow cheese.
After all of the excitement, the two got to the ground,
With a *thud* on the path where there was a bloodhound,
Then Penny said, "Instead of a mouse let's have a bloodhound, like this one on the ground."
With all the commotion, the monster set out,
To find its next victim in the direction of south,
After the mouse went, Jess said,
"I like your thinking, Penny. Now let's go inside.
Because instead of talking we could be staying up late and drinking fizzy pop."

Jessica Atkin (9)
Edge Hill Junior School, Stapenhill

Shoposaurus

I was feeling quite creeped out,
After a dream I'd had last night,
It started off quite normal, like any other weekend,
Homework, chores, then playing with friends,
Suddenly Dad said, "We're out of food,"
Mum didn't like shopping, it put her in a mood.
We jumped in the car and drove to Tesco,
I was hoping to buy a game for my Nintendo.
But Mum had other ideas,
Whilst Dad was thinking about buying beers,
Mum gave us all a job to do
Alex pushed the trolley, but I wanted to!
Mum sent me off to aisle four,
"We're running out of cat food and need some more."
As I made my way through the busy shop,
I got a bit distracted by the sweets and fizzy pop.
That's when I heard an almighty *crash!*
It all happened so fast,
I could not believe my eyes, I did not expect.
To see a scaly, gigantic T-rex,
The shelves toppled on the floor,
Was I really seeing a dinosaur?
He roared and stomped, getting closer and closer,
I gasped and froze behind the 'BOGOF' poster

His teeth were yellow and were as sharp as a knife,
I was terrified for my life,
The tall, turquoise T-rex skipped from aisle to aisle.
He immediately looked, and said to me, "In a while,
crocodile."
The birds were singing as the lights flickered on,
"Did you sleep okay?" asked Mum.

Scott Hulland (9)

Edge Hill Junior School, Stapenhill

My River Of Dreams

I dream about dragons and knights being brave,
Of trolls of monster and princesses to save,
Of faraway islands and treasure to find,
Of thunder and whirlwinds, swirling round in my mind.
I dream of fairies and the wishes they grant,
Of enormous grey elephants and little black ants,
Getting lost in the forest and hiding up trees,
Running fast through the meadows,
Being stung by the bees.
I dream of a warm house on a cold, snowy day,
Looking out of my window, so wanting to play,
Of witches and wizards with a book full of spells,
Climbing up trees and ringing the bells,
So, once again I'm in my bed,
Resting down my sleepy head,
Hoping that my dreams tonight,
Are beautiful, kind, happy and bright.
I'll dream with happiness, for when I do,
Who knows, my dreams may even come true!

Emmie Kendrick-Thorpe (9)
Edge Hill Junior School, Stapenhill

Terrifying Teachers

T errifying teachers screaming at me.

"E xciting homework!" they shout.

"R ead your book five times a day."

"R eally, is that your best?

"I think you should have time out."

F rightening, scary teachers.

"Y ou are in big trouble."

"I know what you have done."

"N o! Don't do that!

G o to the headteacher's room."

T oo many teachers looking at me

E very time I close my eyes

A lways shouting

C hasing me around the school

H elp!

E veryone looking at me

R unning away quickly

S uddenly, I wake up. It's only a dream!

Deni Turner (9)

Edge Hill Junior School, Stapenhill

The Explorer From The Number One Snorer!

Tick-tock, tick-tock, the clock strikes eight,
I'm looking forward to arriving at the dream gate,
I finally drift into a deep sleep,
Which I hope will make my heart leap!

Tonight it looks like I'll be an explorer,
That's what happens when you're the number one snorer,
I'm climbing trees and swimming through lakes,
Oh my gosh, it's the golden gate!

Will it open out wide so I can peep right inside?
I see a glimmering shimmer, then something begins to trot,
Wow! The queen of the unicorn land,
Coming to me on the golden sand.

Bing! Buzz! My alarm unfortunately strikes,
Guess I'll have to finish my dream tomorrow night!

Indie-Lila Sawdon (9)
Edge Hill Junior School, Stapenhill

Moving Up

Every night I close my eyes,
I dream of where the future lies,
I worry that the start of the year,
Will bring me back a lot of fear.

Every night I close my eyes,
I dream of where the future lies,
I'm starting school all over again,
But will I remember how to use my brain!

Every night I close my eyes,
I dream of where the future lies,
I worry that my friends will find,
New friends and leave me behind.

Every night I close my eyes,
But I know the future lies
I'm a bit scared but I know it's time,
'Cause at Edge Hill I know I'll be fine.

Sophie Insley (9)
Edge Hill Junior School, Stapenhill

The Flower Dream

I saw you delivered as a bud
I watched you open out
You turned into something good
That made people smile all about.

We took you to your new home
It wasn't certain if your new owner was home
I had to make sure that you would be grown
With lots of love and care.

Now that the end is here
And we know you won't be alone
You don't have anything to fear
So be free and enjoy your new home

You're so colourful and pretty in full bloom
Flowers make people happy and smile
Flowers brighten up every room
Even though they only last a while.

Mya Leigh Sherriff (9)
Edge Hill Junior School, Stapenhill

Shout And The Animal Doubt

Upon this dream is where I stay
As I huddle with the animals and sleep on hay.

Oh, dream, please let me out,
I'm begging you before I shout.
These animals are in such doubt

The fluffy sheepdog
and
The leapy frog

Oh, don't forget about the donkey!
Have you seen him? He's sooo wonky

As I saw the bat soaring,
Well, I found it quite boring

One of my eyes had a little twitch
But then I found out it was a trick.

Thank you, dream, for letting me out.
So I don't have to *shout!*

Eleanor Charlotte Taylor (8)
Edge Hill Junior School, Stapenhill

My Wonderful Unicorn Dream

I'm riding a unicorn all through the town.
When the people see me they give me a frown.
No need for jealousy as you can have one too.
Just follow me and do as I do.
There are unicorns everywhere, even in the sky.
I shout to my unicorn, "Fly, Uni, fly!"
She dances and prances and twirls all around,
Nothing can stop my unicorn now.
As the day comes to an end,
I don't want to go
But my Uni tells me,
"I'll see you tomorrow!"
I whisper, "Bye-bye!"
And give her a hug
Then wake up in bed as snug as a bug.

Isla Mitchell (8)
Edge Hill Junior School, Stapenhill

Remember?

I really can't remember what I dreamt last night
I don't think it was good as I woke up in a fright
I'm not sure if there were monsters or scary things
Don't know if there were vampires with huge back
wings
I'm not sure if there were witches with tall black hats
Don't know if there were lions or other massive cats
There might have been some zombies trying to eat my
brain
There could have been a bomb exploding on a train
There might have been a fire burning, hot and bright
But then I really can't remember what I dreamt last
night.

Jacob Oliver Downie (9)
Edge Hill Junior School, Stapenhill

Panic Room

I'm in a room and stuck
With spiders, just my luck
A panic room should be fun
But from this, I want to run

There are pictures everywhere
Of spiders, so I'm scared
I spot one on the chair
Which makes me itch my hair

He seems so very hairy
Which makes him look so scary
I run and try to hide
But the spider's at my side

I take a closer look
I think he says, "Hi, Brooke!"
I look again and see
He's tiny next to me

And now this is the end.
The spider is my friend.

Brooke Holford (8)
Edge Hill Junior School, Stapenhill

The Monster Who Was Not Scary

Buddy is my monster and he lives under my bed
When I met him last night, was it in my head?
Buddy is blue from head to toe
With four big pink eyes that glow and glow
I love my Buddy Monster,
He will keep me safe at night
Do you think he might hurt me?
Oh no, not even a little bite.
If Buddy wakes me crying
I will just switch on the light
And what do you think will happen next?
Well, Buddy will have a fright!
I love my monster, Buddy, forever day and night
Sweet dreams, Buddy Monster,
You've made my nightmares bright.

Hollie Anna Dowson (9)
Edge Hill Junior School, Stapenhill

The Wonders Of Gorgeous Good Dreams

Good dreams are always fun
I could see you guys last night
Swinging me up to the sky
I could see you guys dancing
You gave me a bit of a fright.

I saw your guys' superpowers
And you also have a magical world
I also saw some rainbow birds
And they also were curled.

I'm having so much fun
I also saw something in the sky
It might have been a bird.
Or it might have also been a fly.

My journey is nearly over now
I just saw a plane
It went as fast as a cheetah
I just felt a drop of rain.

Maria Shamdin (9)
Edge Hill Junior School, Stapenhill

Dancer

The dream has come to me one day
About the dancer so far away.
Beauty shines from her fame,
Olivia was her name
She liked gymnastics and other sports,
But dance was what she liked the most.
She took part in a competition once
And gained a medal for her dance.
Talent was her second nature
And every day was a new adventure.
And then she went to grandad for a visit
Looked at the mirror and said, "What is it?"
The face looked similar, like not the dream
She turned around and there was me.

Natalia Wlodkowska (8)
Edge Hill Junior School, Stapenhill

The Lucky Girl!

There once was a girl,
As kind as an angel,
She once found a pearl,
Whilst swimming in the ocean.

She held it so tight,
So she wouldn't let go,
Not wanting it out of sight,
So she would not have a fright.

The pearl shone like never before,
Because of the rays of the sun,
She knew she would love it forever more,
It felt like it was meant to be.

She could feel it in her tummy,
She felt blessed and loved,
And forever she knew
She would always be lucky.

Ashton Stanley Hawkley (9)
Edge Hill Junior School, Stapenhill

I Had A Dream

Once I had a dream.
That the whole of the world was covered in cream.
Then I saw a goat,
On a boat.
So he decided to gloat on the moat.

In my dream,
Besides the cream,
My dad was being bad.
So he felt sad
But also mad
Although my dad felt really bad, my mum felt glad.

My friend, Lily,
Was very silly,
But Maria,
I wanted to see her,
But she was not near,
I called for her but she could not hear,
And then the tree,
It waved at me!

Charley May Clarke (8)
Edge Hill Junior School, Stapenhill

In My Dreams

In my dreams, I can be whoever I want to be.
A football player lifting the World Cup,
After scoring goals with my amazing right foot.
A superhero fighting crime,
Flying high in the midnight sky.
A deep-sea diver exploring the ocean's bed,
Avoiding sharks that might bite off my head.
An astronaut travelling through space,
Walking on the moon in a slow-moving pace.
In my dreams as strange as they can be,
I can be whoever I want to be.

Finley Brown (9)
Edge Hill Junior School, Stapenhill

Spiders

In my bedroom all alone.
I sit there looking at my phone.
I look at the wall and see,
A spider staring down at me.

It has a big, fat body and spindly legs,
I hope it hasn't laid any eggs.
It begins to move across the wall.
And I run out into the hall.

The next thing I do is scream,
Then I wake up, it was just a dream.
I can't explain how scared I feel,
But I'm so relieved it wasn't real!

Emily Louise West (9)
Edge Hill Junior School, Stapenhill

The Opposite World

Spiders are famous
And fairies are dancing
Footballers flying
Oh, what could be happening?

What's all around me,
And what's under there?
What is this world?
Where is their great mayor?

Oh, what could that be?
Let's go on a chase
But this world is a mess
With things out of place

There's grass up high
And trees down low
Butterflies singing
How far does this go?

Katie Smith (9)
Edge Hill Junior School, Stapenhill

Nightmares

"N ight-time Leo," my nanny said
  I know it's time, so get tucked up in bed
G randad and Nanny said goodnight
H ave you ever seen such a light?
T alking to a clown I had a frown
M aking a funny, strange sound
A s soon as I saw a flash-like beam
R inging bells and the door was bright
E very day I see pitch-white
S oon I woke up and it was just a dream.

Leo Raymond Williams (9)
Edge Hill Junior School, Stapenhill

I Don't Know Why?

I don't know why
I don't know why
I never ever dream at all!

Should I try cheese?
Or it is peas?
Someone help me, please! Oh please!

I don't know why
I don't know why
I never ever dream at all!

I wake up every morning
My sleep is black and boring
Night after night, snoring and snoring

I don't know why
I don't know why
I never ever dream at all!

Emilia Rose Shorthouse (8)
Edge Hill Junior School, Stapenhill

Dancing Dragons!

Once there was a dancing dragon,
That thought he was good at dancing,
He wasn't very good at all,
In fact, it looked like he was prancing.

He entered a dancing competition.
And the audience laughed and laughed,
I went up to help him,
Because he was dancing daft.

The audience cheered and clapped,
And you should have seen his face,
He was used to coming last,
But instead, we won first place.

Joe Shaw (8)
Edge Hill Junior School, Stapenhill

Mermaids

I saw a mermaid in the sea,
I wish she was swimming with me.
Then I met a magical fish,
That said I could have a wish.

I asked him for a tail, all bright.
To help me swim all day and night.
The mermaid's hair was long and curly,
And her pretty tail was very swirly.

She was singing a happy song,
Which lasted all day long.
When it was time to say goodbye,
I thought that I was going to cry.

Gwen Jacquest (9)
Edge Hill Junior School, Stapenhill

Food

I had a dream about some food
It put me in a very good mood
My dream was of lots of treats
So the first thing I saw was sweets.

Then I ate some lovely dairy
That probably came from the chocolate fairy
In my dream, I ate a cake
That was shaped like a wriggly snake.

I saw a lady with a sweetie trolley
So I bought a big red lolly
Now my dream is really done
I just have time for one more bun.

Harry Jacquest (9)
Edge Hill Junior School, Stapenhill

Dinosaur

D inosaurs are everywhere, what shall I do?

I think I should run out, where should I go to?

N owhere is safe, they are closing in on us

O h! What luck, it's the Fortnite battle bus!

S afe at last as we soar into the sky

A aaargh! I've been sniped. I think I'm going to die!

U rgent! Urgent! I need help from my team!

R elax, it's all over. It was only a dream.

Ted Drake (9)
Edge Hill Junior School, Stapenhill

Let's Play Football!

"**F** ynn Briscoe takes it wide."

"**O** h wow, what a goal!"

"**O** ver the defender's wall and the keeper watched it roll."

T he keeper watched it roll

B ecoming a footballer

A nd playing on television

L ike my dad has done before

L ive for all to see

E very Saturday, playing the game

R unning around as fans cheer my name.

Fynn Briscoe (8)
Edge Hill Junior School, Stapenhill

Princess

P lease give me dreams where I play all day
R emembering
I n the palace where I have to stay
N ight-time can be scary, or so it may seem
C an my dreams become a reality?
E verlasting games with friends I play
S ometimes dreams can stay with me
S haring memories of my princess dreams with sunshine rays.

Faith Bosch (9)
Edge Hill Junior School, Stapenhill

Rainbow Unicorns

I rode a rainbow unicorn
We rode across the sky
I fed her lots of Skittles
Because they make her fly.
We shot off like a rocket
As I kissed my diamond locket
The clouds were bright and colourful
They sparkled, shimmered and shone
Now it's time say goodnight, my rainbow unicorn
I hope to see you tomorrow
When daylight turns into night.

Courtney Kelly (9)
Edge Hill Junior School, Stapenhill

The Future

T he people walking, filled with glee
H overing above the sky is me
E verything is now robotic

F loating cars are so hypnotic
U nderground is what used to be,
T he last few signs of history
U pside down is how we sleep
R eading books about caves that are deep
E veryone loves the future.

Molli Rose Walker (9)
Edge Hill Junior School, Stapenhill

Twinkle Twinkle Little Star

Twinkle twinkle little star
How I wonder what I will be.
A doctor, teacher, or even a vet?
But for now, I will have to wait and see.

When the sun goes down
And lie in my bed.
Dreams of what I can be
Spin around in my head.

Then a bright spark,
Appears in the dark,
And an image of me appears
At work in the park.

Renee Upton (9)
Edge Hill Junior School, Stapenhill

My Dog, Bailey

Me and my dog Bailey, missing each other
Making space in our hearts to remember one another
All the happy times we spent together in our lives
I will remember you until the end of time
But we know we all have dark times
We cannot stop them creeping
But I'll always be there for you, Bailey
Even though you're sleeping.

Alexis Johnson (9)
Edge Hill Junior School, Stapenhill

Tales On The Sea

As I close my eyes to sleep
I see the sea so blue and deep.
A cruise ship is where I dream to be.
Having fun in the sun and playing with everyone.
Meeting up with other ships, making friends.
Telling tales of pirate ships and big whales.
A Jolly Roger flag in the distance, I see.
Oh no! I hope it's not coming for me!

Honour Raine Isom-Dunn (9)
Edge Hill Junior School, Stapenhill

Nightmares!

Spooky stares
Spooky nightmares

Who's in the cave
With me and my mum?

Is it a beast?
Am I his feast?

I need to escape
I am so scared

I heard his roar
It sounded like a snore

It made me jump
I banged my head
Oh no! It's okay, I'm in my bed.

Alfie Winson (9)
Edge Hill Junior School, Stapenhill

Close Your Eyes And Dream

Close your eyes my little one.
Close your eyes and dream.
You can be anyone,
Anyone you dream.
You can go anywhere,
Do anything,
Be anyone,
Just close your eyes
And dream your dream, your dreams...

Samaira Anwar (9)
Edge Hill Junior School, Stapenhill

Star

Roses are red,
Violets are blue,
No words can describe how much I miss you
In another land far away,
Which is where you'll have to stay,
Although I wish I could have one more day,
Happy hearts have died away on this dreadful day
I miss the way you used to play.

A special someone,
Lost at heart,
I have loved you from the very start,
Caring and quiet, yes that's you,
Everything about you is so true
Soft fur, twinkling knowing eyes,
All these words used to describe,
Some bunny so special, I pause to sigh,
A simple nudge just once more,
Is that too much to ask for?

Amazing like me,
Loving and kind,
Important memories fly to mind,
Careful but childish,
Excellent in so many ways

My little star as bright as day,
My emotions are starting to play,
My tears have fallen, a lot of them too,
I would give anything for another day or hour,
But I will have to wait as I let you fade away.

To me you are amazing, you know that is true,
I just want another endless hug with you
You chased the cats all around,
Just like a silly clown
On Saturday I was told,
Then I let our pages unfold,
Forever in my heart, you will stay,
In my heart, until I fade away.

Roses are red,
Violets are blue,
Alice, my bunny,
I love you!

Keezia Mya Evans (11)
Grange Primary School, Bainbridge Green

Unicorn Dream

Mrs Unicorn, I can see my unicorns flying in the air,
I am with magical creatures in my dream,
I am in a soft play area with a unicorn and it has a
magical sky.
I feel excited that I am with my favourite unicorn,
We fly around the rainbows on my unicorn,
I can see magic under the rainbow,
Unicorns can fly as high as possible
Also, I had a secret unicorn
I once had a secret unicorn that lived under my bed.
And it had magical powers to be invisible
And when she saw someone
She turned back to a teddy bear
I also had a cat
Once upon a time, there was a cat called Bella
And she was lost
And one day someone found her
And trained her as a house pet
They took her on as their very own
And made her friendly to others
When they came and stroked her
So they took Bella around the street
So that everyone could see her
And they smiled like it was yesterday

That black and white cat was born in the city
There were no trees or gardens near her home
Only an avenue of streetlights and paving stones
Strewn with dirt, blown up by the passing traffic
Midnight was the safest time
For a black and white cat.

Ebony Mai Forbes (8)
Grange Primary School, Bainbridge Green

The Necroquake!

I fell into a deep sleep and travelled to Shyish
Falling through reality itself
The first face I saw was the Great Nagash
I was surprised to be back in the realm of death.

Nagash said to me in a grim voice
"The Mortarch of Death is dead, his skull was smashed,
I want you to take his place.
That means you start the necroquake."

"But I am no necromancer your greatness!"
He started to mutter a spell
He gave me the power of necromancy
And I began to shred reality

I was overjoyed to be invited to a black coach
My new army raged terror in the realm of chaos
We overthrew in a matter of hours
I was somewhat disappointed when I awoke.

Issac Wheelden (11)
Grange Primary School, Bainbridge Green

Lost...

G rowling wolves follow me in the dead of night
E nd is near
T he clock is ticking
T he house is nearby
I 'm running of time
N ever getting lost again
G oodbye

L ikely staying here on my sofa
O nly see
S taying in bed
T omorrow

I nside this climax
N ew threats may appear

T he end just might be near
H ow may I go home
E ver again?

W ould you take a peek?
O r let them sleep?
O n the hilltop
D ark as the night sky
S ilently creeping, very sly.

Phoebe Longden (10)
Grange Primary School, Bainbridge Green

The Nightmare

I escorted my dogs to a breath-taking location
They trundled around in the lush, extensive grass
Max trotted a bit too far, I had to catch up.
There he was, distant to a park
I put Max and Quill on the lead
I started to walk my dogs home but then I heard a...
Creak! I rotated my head like The Flash
The wind started to whistle
A clown appeared, then he started to chase
My heart was pumping
This wasn't fun
So me and my dogs began to run
I tried to hide my dogs
Near a pile of logs
Then they vanished
I closed my eyes
To my surprise, I was in bed
My dogs were asleep on the floor curled up in a ball...

Jessica Cartwright (10)
Grange Primary School, Bainbridge Green

Sleepover Party

S ome friends come to stay,

L ate when you go to sleep,

E ndless fun,

E ndless laughter,

P illow fight and popcorn.

O pening doors whilst screaming, so you're getting in trouble

V imto and other drinks all around

E verlasting movies, well, that's what it feels like

R udeness, no!

P arties may be included

A fter what you've done in the day you're desperate to get there,

R unning around like maniacs,

T o and fro,

Y ou'll get so excited!

Ava Mae Hess (9)
Grange Primary School, Bainbridge Green

The Clown!

Noises began to frighten me
I opened my eyes to see
My friends watching me
Shimmering light came from the river
We went to see
Scared to death, we saw a clown
And began to run speedily
If I wasn't careful our life would be done!

As we thought we'd lost him
We went into my tent
But two minutes later
I turned around to see
A clown watching me
I froze, I couldn't move as she said,
"I'll kill you!"
I woke up screaming
Thank God it was all a dream.

Lucy Medlicott (10)
Grange Primary School, Bainbridge Green

Nightmare!

N o one's with me in this house

I creep downstairs

G oing to the back door

H olding back like a runner about to sprint... Should I go out?

T ime is essence

M y worst fear is realised - creepy-crawly clown zombies

A fter dark shivers start going through your spine

R eally horror-struck, I think, *will this ever end?*

E very night I have the same dream, sometimes I think, *could it come true?* Yes! And it did the next night.

Samuel Marsh (11)
Grange Primary School, Bainbridge Green

Castle In The Distance

W orrying about where I could be

O ver the clouds or underneath the sea

N oon was the time where we saw it glow

D own the path, finding a way that made me say, "Woah!"

E erie eyes glowing in the midnight light

R ight near the castle, something wasn't right

L ate that night, I gave her a pat, reassuring

A n apprehensive look on Eleanor's face

N ever again at that pace

D rifting away back to our homes.

Kia Louise Roberts (11)
Grange Primary School, Bainbridge Green

Magical Dream

M agical dreams come true
A mazing things can happen
G iant castle full of excitement
I n a wonderful world of happiness
C ascading waterfalls made of chocolate
A nything can happen
L eprechauns guarding the vibrant rainbows

D are to believe in hopes and desires
R eality is so far away
E verything is as perfect as can be
A wesomeness is everywhere in
M y dreams.

Poppy Asterley (9)
Grange Primary School, Bainbridge Green

The Dead!

N othing is as strange as this. The moon smiling evilly

I open my eyes, petrified as I can be

G lancing forwards, all I see is red liquid

H ow can this be?

T hunder boomed, something moved

M y worst fear has come, a terrifying, creepy zombie

A ll I see is blood, blood, blood

R unning as fast a cheetah, it kills

E ating my neighbour

S uddenly, I open my eyes and wake up in my bed.

Phoebe Olivia Jervis (11)
Grange Primary School, Bainbridge Green

My Parents

Normally Mum and Dad work their socks off
I love them for what they do.
Dad works at B&M and Mum works at home.
But in my dreams, they switched roles
As Dad steals stale biscuits from the secret stash and
the tin goes *bang!*
Where Mum is at B&M working for cash, isn't she glad.
When she comes home
She found the house is a tip, she found make-up on the
boys
Trousers and shirts and aftershave on the girls.

Thomas Marsh (11)
Grange Primary School, Bainbridge Green

Nightmares

C loudy nightmare
L ove or hate
"**O** w!" I screamed
W ow, it's after me
N ow run away
S irens to be heard.

As the scary clown approached
I pushed him away
They followed me every day
A masked man,
I wonder why?
Maybe he's ugly.

Nathan Derrick Colin Woodhouse (11)
Grange Primary School, Bainbridge Green

Fabulous Fortnite

F abulous Fortnite

O vercrowding

R unning as fast as Turbo the snail

T ilted Towers is my favourite place

N utters shooting at my face

I diots hiding, playing dead

T here is the best character

E xperts are the worst cheaters.

Matthew Harry Lloyd (11)

Grange Primary School, Bainbridge Green

Creepy Clowns

C reepy clowns, sneaky like blood-curdling mice with little eyes

L isten to heavy footsteps and cloudy minds

O ften outrageous clowns follow me every day

W hen I'm alone and scared

N ightmares with clowns, horrifying

S cary, scary clowns wherever I go.

Emily Erin Moreton (11)
Grange Primary School, Bainbridge Green

St James' Park

S inging alone
T he crowd roaring

J umping
A lmirón
M isses the target
E veryone groaning
S adly

P laying City
A way
R afa the gaffer says
"**K** eeper will stay."

Jaydn Gary Phillip James Peart (10)
Grange Primary School, Bainbridge Green

Violence

Very strange things happened
Innocent people are actually spies
John Wick the hitman can handle them
Like a lion hunting its prey,
Bang! He took the first shot with the combat shotgun,
John punched and kicked while the violin player,
Shot with the SP-L pistol.

Cameron Philip Cotton (11)
Grange Primary School, Bainbridge Green

Beautiful Butterfly

A cinquain

Unique
A butterfly
That sings so gracefully
Its enchanted wings flap with pride
Unique.

Jolie Amber Lily Phillips (11)
Grange Primary School, Bainbridge Green

Roblox

A haiku

Funny games to play
Playing with friends that you know
With laughter and joy.

Layla Evans (9)
Grange Primary School, Bainbridge Green

Green

A haiku

See khaki fly by,
All green except feeling blue,
Customary rise.

Charlie Farmer (11)
Grange Primary School, Bainbridge Green

The Filthy Rich Life

F aith is always around me. I always succeed in everything

I own more gold than the president, bills I can always afford

L ife is easy, all you need is a friend, a cute dog

T ea parties I hold with cakes and milkshakes

H ouse parties are always held at my house

Y ou think that I have only one house, but I have eight

R ed carpets every day. Private jets and four yachts. Twenty-four villas I own

I own twenty-nine supercars, Lamborghinis, Bugattis. I even own helicopters

C hocolate companies are the best, well, mine is way better

H ow do you get rich, you ask? Well, you simply do something *spectacular!*

Maddison Ford (10)
Hazel Slade Primary Academy, Hazel Slade

Performing As A Ballerina

I felt uneasy, my knees felt weak, and my mouth was
dry.
I thought, *I need to calm down, the time is already here
and it's all about to unwind,*
I carefully tied on my pointe shoes and tiptoed onto the
stage,
Then the piano music started and went at a slow pace.
I started to prance from left to right and the audience
thought that was a beautiful sight
The dim light shone onto my face and made me lose
my place
But then I got back up again as the curtains
Closed and done was another show.

Hollie Rachel Eileen Timms (10)
Hazel Slade Primary Academy, Hazel Slade

Football Mad!

Peep, peep, the whistle blew.
We scored a goal, oh yay! Oh phew!
They scored a goal (we never win!)
I wished to put that team in the bin!

It was half-time, we've changed sides now!
It is 3-1, I don't know how!
We scored a goal! We are going to win!
One of the other teams kicked me in the shin!

The second half soon began,
Quickly down the field, I ran!
As the goalie kicked the ball up high,
I headed it in, the other team were like, why?

Ezra Nathaniel Davies (8)
Hazel Slade Primary Academy, Hazel Slade

Super Gang

S upervillains there are, all around me in the big, big city

U nder, on top, they're just not disappearing

P unching their way towards me and my friends

E verything hurting in my head

R ico and Luco feeling the same

G rass lifts up into the air

A nd there, is a super gang

N othing can stop them here and now

"G o to bed," they say to me

S uper Gangs are the best!

Vinny Coxon (10)
Hazel Slade Primary Academy, Hazel Slade

My Big Dream!

Life in a dream
Is a magical thing.

Gymnastics is my dream
And I try not to go
Wrong in anything.

It's a competition
Oh wow, very exciting
But no worries, I'm
Amazing at anything.

Everyone will be there
You named it, my nan, mom
They are there.

I'm so excited,
It's so delighful.

Amelia Harrison (10)
Hazel Slade Primary Academy, Hazel Slade

Gamer Land

G amer Land is crazy
A nd everyone here is lazy.
M y land is incredible
E ven though it's not edible.
R oblox, Minecraft and more.

L ots of people never got bored
A nd it is the best
N ot the rest.
D rawing people is the best.

Matthew Peakman (10)
Hazel Slade Primary Academy, Hazel Slade

Show Dog

S how dogs are wonders,
H ow did you know?
O ver the beam, they go,
W onderful tricks are their favourite thing,

D ogs are cute and show dogs are cool,
O ver, wow!
G o, go show dog.

Caitlan Haywood (9)

Hazel Slade Primary Academy, Hazel Slade

Dream

D reams can be beautiful

R oblox is the best

E very day people have dreams

A nd animals have dreams

M onsters, animals, history and lots of things.

Daniel Tonks (10)

Hazel Slade Primary Academy, Hazel Slade

The Treacherous Nightmare!

He! He! He!
It's you again I see.
Like a pack of wolves desperately calling,
The killer clown yelled, "You looked appalling!"
I took no notice, he was very wrong.
It felt like I'd been there for too long.

Although I behaved the best that I could,
It took me back to my childhood.
A blanket full of nails pinned me down.
This was because of the killer clown.
In the sky, evil clouds grinned at me.
Effortlessly, a barbaric male was a stinging bee.

Nightmare! Nightmare! What have I done?
I want to be lit up by the sun.
Exhausted my body shook,
There was one thing I shouldn't have taken.
I regret what I did,
Somewhere I could've hidden.

Hurry up! Call Mum and Dad!
By far, this is the worst nightmare I have ever had.
Just wake up, let me be at home,
It is like I am trapped inside a dome.

Mum? Dad? Are you here?
The killer clown whispered in my ear...

Hollie Hunter (10)

Hollinswood Primary School, Hollinswood

The Isolated Girl

As I gracefully drifted to sleep,
All of a sudden I started to plunge deep.
Splash!
I got out the water I had no cash.

All I could see was the thick, opaque smoke,
I hoped it was a joke.
Alarmingly, I smelt the rotten, revolting blood,
There was an unknown ghost with a hood.

As the ruby-red sun started to set,
Petrifying, it got very wet.
As I walked around, I knew I was in the deep, dark woods,
Frighteningly, I stepped in revolting blood.

As the branches cried
The wind blew by
Clouds were the sea waving
Like silly children, the emerald land was misbehaving.

As I noticed no one was around,
The isolated girl
Terrifyingly I could hear a creepy sound.
As I walked closer, it went as quiet as a mouse,
Suddenly, there was an abandoned house.

Phoebe Willis (10)
Hollinswood Primary School, Hollinswood

The Light

As I drifted into my tranquil sleep,
When I awoke, I gave a leap.
Slowly, the aroma of flesh filled the air
Then an old woman gave me a pear.

Cautiously, I started opening my eyes,
After I heard these voices telling me lies.
Like a waterfall a tear fell down my cheek,
Argh! As a bright light gave me a freak.

Like a lion waiting for my prey,
Suddenly, I began walking the other way.
Splash! As the blood dropped,
While I was walking to my spot.

Above my head was a line,
By now I knew I was running out of time.
Rapidly, I slid my hand across the wall,
The rough blood made me fall.

It was a nightmare as the blood rushed down,
After that I gave a frown.
Yelling and screaming for my life,
A cloaked man came behind me with a knife...

Kamilya Sharif (9)
Hollinswood Primary School, Hollinswood

The Day I Became An Actress

Beep! Beep! Beep! Beep!
At the crack of dawn, I elegantly woke up,
To receive a beagle pup.
Suddenly, my old, overjoyed servant gave me a dress,
And said, "Go get dressed, you look a mess."
Snap!

After I put the dress on, money kept glaring at me,
I thought I was going crazy.
Why am I putting this on?
"Since you are going on the red carpet, (Bon Bon)!"
Snap!

My ivory dress shone like a diamond in the sky.
It made me feel very shy.
Later the sun danced at me strangely,
When I was pacing bravely.
Snap!

On the red carpet, I wore ruby-red lipstick,
Where I felt homesick.
This must be a delusion.
It was causing confusion.
Snap!

Daisy Louise Morris (10)
Hollinswood Primary School, Hollinswood

The Future Is Real!

Bang! Crash!
Cautiously, I sat up, peering out of my window,
Like flash, I glanced behind me.
Where are my friends? They were not there,
Why did they not stop to care?

Like lightning, my eyes widened to see a rusty tree waving at me.
Furiously, I sprinted to my ancient calendar.
The year was 3033. Wow!
Could this mean I was in the future?

Carefully, I went to find my clothes,
Oh no! There are loads.
Like mould, the scent was dreadful.
All I could see was rust, rust, rust.

Like a racing car, I went to the door.
Quickly, I found my friends.
"Hello over there, remember me"
The future was real!

Oh well, they probably didn't since it was 3033.

Brooke Marie Benevento (10)
Hollinswood Primary School, Hollinswood

Fortnite Invasion

Swoosh!
As we entered the game,
We had to jump off the train.
As we rapidly landed,
We saw a variety of people.

Anxiously, me and Kane were killing people,
We were on a team,
Waiting for our big dream.
Rapidly, we got more kills
Showing off our skills.
I could taste victory.

Boom!
Like a raging bull, we neutralised a squad
Whilst on a quad.
I could smell the rotten flesh,
We used a lot of our mesh.
I could feel the metal on the gun.

Like a raging bull, we defeated a duo,
Me and Kane wrecked many people.
In the distance, we heard gunshots,
There were so many bots.
I could see build battles.

Eesa Faisal (10)
Hollinswood Primary School, Hollinswood

Nightmare Forever!

Cushion, keep me away,
From this malevolent man.
He's hurting me like a vicious lion,
Rapidly, I was drenched in vermilion blood.

Like a barbaric elephant, he barged passed me,
Ouch!
Slowly, my eyes were about to open,
Nightmare, nightmare, what have I done?

Swiftly my nose inhaled anger,
Meanwhile, the sluggish man glared into my soul.
Suddenly, like a raging bull, my veins pulsated,
Nightmare, nightmare, call Mum and Dad.

This could be the end,
"Mum! Dad!" Like a baby, I sobbed.
"Hello, it's nice to see you again,
Your life is going to end soon."

Holly Reed (9)
Hollinswood Primary School, Hollinswood

The Games

As I slept like a buoyant baby,
I drifted to my heavy sleep.
Suddenly, I leapt off my ruby-red and crimson bed,
To see my oceanic chair wave at me.

Bop! Slash! Sizzle!
The action is half a fraction,
I could smell the scent of the food that got cooked.
I could see the action that was violent.

Bang! Kapow! Sizzle!
The machine is a skyscraper,
I could have the aroma.
However, my monitor is a waterpark of joy.

Like a raging bull,
I had raged because I had died.
It was amusing but I could taste
The victory on the tip of my long and thick tongue.

Evrim Randa (10)
Hollinswood Primary School, Hollinswood

Loyal Rises

As I effortlessly drifted into my peaceful slumber,
My eyes glared at the polished palace.
I couldn't believe my azure eyes,
Shockingly, I was going to be king.

When I got to my destination, I was in a limousine,
I could see my luxurious throne.
As I got out of the limousine, everyone cheered,
Like a big mist, the gleaming glitter rained down on
me.

As slow as a snail, I sat on the bloodshot throne,
The sizzling sun shone on the scarlet throne.
Everyone went silent like a statue,
When I said my speech, they put the luscious crown on
me.
Yay! Yay! Yay!

Jake Weston (10)
Hollinswood Primary School, Hollinswood

The Lost But Not Found!

Swiftly, the plane began to zoom,
My veins pulsated. *Boom!*
I could smell the jets straight away,
As quick as a flash, the plane flew down.

As I effortlessly woke up,
There was no one there, only me.
My hands were a washing machine,
the mountains were dissolving in tears.

As I absently got up and tripped over,
The trees laughed at me.
My stomach rumbled,
I quietly moaned with dejection.

I could feel the smoke explore me,
The taste of salt numbed my tongue.
Crack! I felt the plane disintegrate,
My head was a drum.

Mia Crofts (10)
Hollinswood Primary School, Hollinswood

Fortnite Invasion

Swoosh!
The verdant grass swayed side to side,
Me and Eesa briskly glared at it.
And it gave us a fearful, "Hello!"

In this spine-chilling and hair-raising,
Location called Haunted Hills.
Vigilantly, lurking down below are
Perplexing body parts.
Shaking the ground like an uncontrollable
Earthquake.
Crack!

Sluggishly, risen from the dead,
A sinister skull trooper.
Rapidly, I felt goosebumps rise.
His arms were claws.

I could taste victory.
As quick as a flash, a chalky arm fell.
Eesa!

Kane Young (10)
Hollinswood Primary School, Hollinswood

I Wish I Was Royalty!

As I fell into a deep sleep,
I suddenly woke up and looked at my feet.
I had rose-gold shoes on,
Before I could call my mom.

Quickly like a raging bull,
I glanced at my room, it seemed quite full.
The throne smirked at me,
While the crown winked, *did you see?*

And so I called Mom,
I ran with slippers on,
Shouting louder, more and more.
Come on now, I'll bring a saw!

Vroom! I ran to the closet,
All these clothes are under deposit.
As the stained glass started to cry,
I gave a huge sigh.

Nadusha Iyne (10)
Hollinswood Primary School, Hollinswood

Doll Vs Death

Tick-tock! Tick-tock!
Hurry up, the time is running away from us.
Like a raging bull, a creepy, cramped doll charged at me,
She snatched her rotten, bloody, steel knife out of her pocket.

I could smell the revolting stench of rotting blood on her knife,
Is this going to be the end of my ten-year life?
Her bulging, brown eyes were golf balls staring at me,
I wish I could escape this misery.

Slice!
I heard the petrifying doll murder the people of Hollinswood
But then she found me and trapped me in a corner,
Help me!

Tia Biram (10)
Hollinswood Primary School, Hollinswood

Dragon Ball

As I glanced into his demon eyes,
He was charging like a shooting star.
He showed no respect.
"Help! I can't touch him."

Flash! I charged up,
As ultra instinct powered up,
Uncomfortably his head turned upside down,
His mighty muscles burst.

I could feel the flames,
Burning my skin like a crisp.
Since he did his final move,
"Kamehameha!"

I stood before him,
My final chance
Boom! Crack!
We lay on the floor, out of energy.

Conrad Babane (10)
Hollinswood Primary School, Hollinswood

Magical Unicorns

As the crimson sunset went down.
The submerged clouds engulfed me.
Darkness fell towards me,
The sky was a pitch-black painting.

Quietly, I could sense the unicorn's crystal-blue eyes.
The frantic eyes harshly stared at me.
Boom!
That was the sound of mysterious animals.

As the blazing sun came up, it inspired the ivory
unicorn,
The sun was a torch burning my skin.
The unicorn's eyes were like crystal diamonds.
I saw the enchanting clouds - they were as white as
stars.

Ciara Priede-Wilson (9)
Hollinswood Primary School, Hollinswood

Wreck

Slowly as I fall into a deep sleep
I begin to dream.
It's different, what is this?

Why is the school not the same?
It is a wrecking ball. Looking for writing.

My heart is jumping like a kangaroo.
Slowly, I walk towards the door.

As steady as a cow.
I look around,
Mati and Liam are there.
As quick as a cheetah,
They say, "Have you been bitten?"
I'm confused, what could they mean?
Mati went to the cupboard and got a baseball bat...

Buddy Powell (9)
Hollinswood Primary School, Hollinswood

Help

As the sparkling, ruby-red sun settled down,
My veins started to pulsate.
The sky was a painted picture,
That was glaring back at me.

Out of nowhere, I could smell blood travel past me.
As I could see blue bullet eye's staring at me.
Before I knew it,
I could feel a bitter-cold breath tickle my neck.

Like a diamond,
My eyes glistened.
Like a raging bull.
My heart raced to my stomach.
Then a single tear escaped my eye.
Help...

Alfie Raymond Ferguson (9)
Hollinswood Primary School, Hollinswood

Bedtime Bombs

As I fell into my peaceful slumber,
My dream began.
In the distance, I could see the mountains wink at me
The rotting blood emanated to my nostrils.

Smell the blood rain.
Ever escape, hang on a chain.
Rapidly, the bomb rolled towards me.
Viciously, the whips spring out of me
Like a lion catching its prey.

Shockingly, the blood rushes down the floor.
It looks like a corpse.
Best explore
The seashore.

Jeenna-Faith Trueman (10)
Hollinswood Primary School, Hollinswood

Evil Circus

I fell into my peaceful dream,
Suddenly, I was in a nightmare.
Magma-red clouds towered over me,
Why am I in a circus?

I couldn't believe my eyes,
Slowly, a dreadful scent of poisonous candyfloss,
Reached my rose.
My heart was pounding like a drum,
Like a flash, I started to run.

Marcel Starszewski (9)
Hollinswood Primary School, Hollinswood

The Winner

We are queueing in the tunnel,
Then I hear the shouts and screams,
The tunnel widens,
The crowd leans.

We walk out past the glamorous, golden trophy.
Hoping to lift it high and proud,
And see the opposition cry in failure,
And the fans shouting nice and loud.

When I see that kick-off is nearing,
The fans cheer,
Drip, slurp, gulp,
Drinking their beer.

At half-time,
Losing 33-6,
Let's hope we can make a comeback,
Even though we're defending like a bunch of sticks.

There are two seconds left,
I get the ball and run fast,
One, two, three, four
Bulking defends, five defenders,
Have been done.
Try! And the kick's over.

We lifted the trophy and proud,
Saw the opposition cry,
In failure, and the fans shouted nice and loud.

George Halstead (10)
John Wilkinson Primary School, Broseley

Right Into The Net!

As I step onto the football pitch
The referee blows the whistle
The enormous size of the football pitch
Makes me feel so little.

I race the ball along the grass
Beaming ear-to-ear with glee
And then an opposing player comes
And gets the ball off me!

He runs away grinning
And laughing with delight
I stand and sulk, not knowing
It's all just a dream in the night!

My teammate comes and comforts me
He says, "Come on, we're here to have fun!"
But then, the ref stops the game
The first half is done.

Second half, I step on
I feel stronger than ever
I'm not going to give up
Never, never, never!

At my feet, I have the ball
Getting close to the goal
I get as near as I can get
And kick the ball right into the net!

Joshua Lowe (10)
John Wilkinson Primary School, Broseley

The Clown!

It was a normal day, my friends were like, "Hey!"
Until we heard a squeak and then we looked a peek to find...
A *clown!*

It made us shudder, it made us frown, it made us clutch, it made us down.
It made me consider, consider an idea, the one that popped in my brain was pretty queer.
The thought was to capture, capture the clown, but all my friends, they weren't down.

So I asked my nan. She was like, "Yay!" So she even bought a frying pan!
We trod in the woods one step at a time to suddenly discover his weird mime.
We collected the net and threw it on him, took off his mask to find out it was...
Ronald McDonald!

I couldn't trust my eyes! I chatted to him and asked for his name and he told me, "Jim," and gave me a *cheeseburger!*

Ethan Arch (10)
John Wilkinson Primary School, Broseley

Unicorns And Me

I was exploring my favourite place, Imagination World,
Where the rain pours with glitter,
And not a single place has
A single piece of litter.

I then realised I was lost in a creepy, sickening,
Wood, and there was not a single path,
Without a single patch of mud.

It was dark, full of tree bark.
I tried to hide,
Like a bear in his lair.

Then I heard a shimmering, glittering sound,
And wondered what could it be?
I looked up and there stood
A unicorn, as beautiful as could be.

Her horn was glimmering and
I was going to stay close to her until dawn.

From then I've had so many adventures
With my friend, and we'll love each other,
Until the end.

Darcey Phillips (10)
John Wilkinson Primary School, Broseley

The Night Of The Earthquake!

All around me all I can see
Are beautiful blossom trees
And flowers that gleam
When the moonlight shows
And the sun goes down.

The petals glitter and the flowers glow.
The creatures appeared and so did the stars
They're all so wonderful
And I had no fear so I walked near
But the ground started to shake!

It was an earthquake
I was so scared I grabbed hold of a tree
I screamed and shouted
As the earthquake got bigger
I let go of the tree, a huge mistake and fell backwards
into a lake!

I shut my eyes tight and the earthquake stopped.
I opened my eyes and I was back at home
I sat up in my bed, and realised,
It was a nightmare, and I'm glad it was over!

Hollie Parfitt (10)
John Wilkinson Primary School, Broseley

I Had A Dream

One day long ago,
I was alone and
And I always had that one dream.
About a Magic Land.
One day...
A cloud came down, down to the ground.
"Hop aboard!" shouted the cloud really loud,
"You won't board and I am proud!" said the cloud...

I hopped on and off we went,
With a whizz and whirl,
Turn and twist up the mountain,
Into the blitz around the corner.
"Do a flip, we're almost there!" screamed the cloud.
As soon as we got there,
My mouth dropped open.

I hopped off the cloud,
To see an amazing place.
With candyfloss carpets!
And rainbow drop roofs,
This place is amazing.

You should come too!

Louisa Mary Evans (10)
John Wilkinson Primary School, Broseley

Baby Dragon

I'm in an egg waiting to hatch,
While I'm watching an exciting football match,
Oh, I really do wish,
That I could be a fish,
And escape this piece of trash,
In just a little flash,
But I'm stuck in this egg.

I'm in an egg waiting to hatch,
The people holding me are playing catch,
I twirl and swirl, I twist and twitch
then I found I was on the ground,
But I'm still stuck in this egg.

So I start to grow,
But my egg says no,
I'm scared and nervous,
Because I'm now in a circus,
Then, *crash!* My egg has turned to mush,
I'm a dragon and that's what I'll be.

Joe Phillips (10)
John Wilkinson Primary School, Broseley

The Olympian's Race

I would like to take part in the Olympics
But it might not come true.
If it does then, who knew?

I will see the crowd
They shall cheer me on
And I shall make my family proud.

I'm waiting to go
Bang!
Off we pop to win the race,
After this, I'll need a brace.

I'm running like a panther, ready to pounce,
My speed builds up, ready to win.
If I don't, my career's in the bin.

I'm almost ready to cross the line
It's like I've almost finished a climb...

I win the race!
All I can hear are whoops and cheers.

Elijah Beau Campbell (9)
John Wilkinson Primary School, Broseley

Police Chase

Call on the radio
Someone speeding
Call the coppers
Stop them wheeling.

Sirens flashing everywhere
Better start running
Or you'll be in despair.

Swerve, skid
Around the corner
More cops join the drama.

Bang! The criminal has crashed
The cops jump out
And give him a bash

"This is the police, get down on the ground!"
Quickly handcuff him with a frown

Put him in the car
Mind your head
Sirens on-off, you go to your cell bed.

Welcome prison
What a shock

Lots of bars
And an officer with a lock.

Joseph Elcock Price Jones (10)
John Wilkinson Primary School, Broseley

Runner's Relief

My dream is to be a runner and it might come true,
And your dream might come true too.
So, I'm racing on the racetrack, slow and fast.
I'm running like a cheetah chasing its prey,
Getting ready to pounce, flying away.
The crowd are cheering me on.
They are as loud as a church bell every night
Giving me a fright that I might not win the running
fight.
When I leg it down the track, I hope I make it back.
I am in the lead like a dog pulling me on a lead.
Now I have won the race and I am feeling ace
And I'm feeling fine and the trophy is mine and I'm
drinking wine.

Harry John Littlewood (9)
John Wilkinson Primary School, Broseley

The Pirates' Poem

The cannons are crawling with fire in the air.
Whilst the mast is whirling in despair,
And the planks are falling with a charge and a prayer.
The pirates are fighting with swords and cries
Looting, grabbing hands in the air.
With a sinking ship and a scare.
It looks like it's the last fight and in the end,
The blues won with a cheer and some beer.
Whilst the pirates are fighting
I managed to sneak a hold of the wheel, flying
Them around with a seal and a squeal.
Whilst we were having a meal.
We all fell and had a hell of a melt
But we all got some chicken pelt.

Max Illingworth (10)
John Wilkinson Primary School, Broseley

Ocean Commotion

The waves are rocking, intimidatingly
Luring me into the sea
As I come onboard the ship
I realise there's only me.

The gloomy sky is surrounding me quickly
As the wind is picking up
Inside me, I'm feeling anxious
Oh, Mom, just pick me up!

I really just hate the ocean
It just causes lots of commotion
I feel like I'm going to sink
Or maybe that's just what I think...
Crash! Splash!
There is just a big flash!

As I get scared I open my eyes
And to my surprise
Everything is still, quiet and calm.

Ellena Hemmings (10)
John Wilkinson Primary School, Broseley

If I Had A Dream

If I had a dream
It would be for me, not you

I wouldn't be a king or queen like Henry III
Or work at a zoo looking after a bird.

I wouldn't be a world record-holder like Wim Hof
Or be an adult that loves crazy golf!

I wouldn't be an author like David Walliams
Or even change my name to Bob Williams.

I wouldn't be a BGT judge like Simon Cowell
Or be the founder of Scouts like Baden Powell.

I wouldn't be a professional sports player using lots of
bats
But... I would live with ten cats!

Luca Piotr Candlin (10)
John Wilkinson Primary School, Broseley

Already A Star

I am dyslexic
I am quite hectic
But my dream is to be a star.
No, not a famous movie star
But a writing, reading, pleasing star,
Yes, a star that shines bright,
Like everyone else.
Sometimes I feel like
I was never meant to come
To this beautiful universe.
But what I realised today is
That I am already a star
An amazing star
That shines brightly
In the magnificent night sky.

If you dream to be a star
Then stay as you are,
Because you already shine
Bright in the night!

Isla Gibb (10)
John Wilkinson Primary School, Broseley

World War Two

M1 Garand getting cocked back
Someone running gets shot in the back.

Bullet cartridges flying everywhere
Better get down or you'll lose your head.

Medics running down the trench
Someone injured on a bench.

No more guns, no more dead.
No more injured on a bed.
We have won the dread.

We thought the Germans would win
But now they're all gone and in the bin.

Thank you all the soldiers who helped us win
We shall remember you every year.

Euan Meek (9)
John Wilkinson Primary School, Broseley

WWII

Jumping out of the plane,
Feeling pain,
Shooting guns,
Time to run,
Pushing forth in the war,
Throwing grenades tall and small,
Jumping in the trench,
What a fall,
Couldn't get any sleep at all
Overhead the planes go by,
I wish that I could fly,
Down go the bombs, whistle and crack,
Ending lives in black,
Annoying rats left and right,
Killing them, giving a fright,
Falling down for the crown,
Saving friends who fall down.

Travis Meek (9)
John Wilkinson Primary School, Broseley

Don't Look Twice

I went into the woods
I looked all around
I saw a tall figure
He had no face and didn't make a sound.

Then he disappeared and so did I
He followed me home to my house, quiet night
Then I was alone, I think
And the sink started dripping
And the power went out.

The next morning I woke up from a scream and shout.
I looked all around
I saw the tall figure
And under my breath
I whispered, "Don't look twice!"

Mollie Eliza Hall (10)
John Wilkinson Primary School, Broseley

Black Arrow Light!

Light as day
Dark as night
No evil shall escape my sight
Beware my power, black arrow light.

The dragon scales are like the galaxies black colour through the night.

Bucky and Willson find a way today to go anywhere
Snotlout, Snotlout, oi, oi, oi.

Coming in hot and blowing out
Snot through the air coming from far, far.

Away from Imagination Land
And from the country
A poem around the world.

Samuel McCreadie (10)
John Wilkinson Primary School, Broseley

When All My Fears Came True...

The stench of rotting food's in the air,
This place seems to be a ghostly lair.

In the sinister dark,
It's as creepy as a shark.

Eeek, creak! I'm gonna take a peek,
At all the dreaded things I seek.

A squeaky, eerie floor,
Surely there can't be more,
I'm pretty sure this is against the law...

My feet are bulky lumps of lead,
I wish I was back in my cosy bed.

Holly Lewis-Dowell (10)
John Wilkinson Primary School, Broseley

The Evil Animals

Creepy, sleepy in my head and then a cat called
Sooty said, "Mua, ha, ha, ha, ha!"
Cobwebs hanging down below, wibbling, wobbling
really slow.

Evil rats, evil bats bouncing around with weird hats.
The evil cats were as crazy as the evil bats
Flying over people's head as they're sleeping in bed.

Up in the attic, your hair goes static
An evil bird was in the attic
Making his feathers flap.

Kira Jones (10)
John Wilkinson Primary School, Broseley

Roof Jumping

Jumping street to street
My high score, I'm trying to beat.

I am all alone
Listening to Post Malone.

Hearing the alarms
Trying to feel calm.

I might fail and get in jail
If I don't bail.

Calling for back up
My friends drinking out of their cups.

I say, "Come here."
Then I hear, "What is it, dear?"

After all, it was a dream.

Ethan Worthington (10)
John Wilkinson Primary School, Broseley

Planets And The Stars

Planets that whirl and twirl
Planets that align and are divine
Planets that are blue, red and green.

The planets stars are glistening like a diamond
All the stars go *boom, boom, boom!*
Every star dances in the sky.

The stars always orbit around Mars
There are always lots more galaxies to explore
But for now, I'll sit down on the floor.

Amelia Burgess (10)
John Wilkinson Primary School, Broseley

Boss The Boxer

A boxer dog barking like a leader trying to not get
fleas.
Then I looked for some trees

Then found a cruise ship and sailed across the seas.
I see my French bulldog friend and all he does is *woof*,
woof and *woof*.

Now I have a home, I now feel company and happiness
inside me.

Jude Baxter (10)
John Wilkinson Primary School, Broseley

The Volcano

Boom!
Bash!
Crash!
Shake it!

Sounds like an earthquake
Bits of turf flying here and there
What a mess
Better run or you'll lose your hair!
Go to the shop to make it stop
Then buy some cider to make it tidier.

William Satchwell (10)
John Wilkinson Primary School, Broseley

Dream Adventure

On my way, I met a huge man smiling at me
I was wondering, *who is he?*
He uttered, "Make a wish, one, two, three!"
I replied, "Will you grant it all for me?"

I wish I can play football with the dolphins
Found myself underwater, trying hard to be a
goalkeeper
The dolphins made a lot of points
What I had were aching joints!

I wish I could play tag with the monkeys up the tree
I was full of energy running after a monkey
I did backflips, somersaults, monkey bar
And caught some monkeys so far.

I wish I can do skateboarding in the clouds
Sliding over a rainbow, screaming loud
I skateboard high and low, having fun as I go
I flipped, I jumped, twisted and bumped my head
Only to find myself in bed.

Angelo Rafael Leuterio Damalerio (8)
St Mary's Catholic Primary School, Madeley

The Magical Land Of Fairies

F lattering fairies in the sky
A nimals in danger, why can't you see?
I ncredible fairies come to save the day
R ed, multicoloured fairies always get their way
I ncredible ice, this is so cool
E xciting fairies, they are so warm
S aving the day is incredible.

F luttering their wings as they fly in the sky
A nimals are in danger in the kingdom
I ncredible powers, the fairies discover
R eady to go and protect the rainforest
I see the fairies help the animals, building walls to stop the poacher
E veryone in the kingdom is safe and happy
S aving the day, keeping danger away is the new job of the fairies.

Happy fairies fluttering high
Beautiful sunshine in the sky
The land of fairies is magical
What happens there is wonderful
The fairies help loads of people
This is why it is wonderful

Incredible creatures are everywhere
Unknown to the fairies, they have magic to share.

Summer Lucy Grace Jones (8)
St Mary's Catholic Primary School, Madeley

Darkness

I have a different dream every night.
Last night, I found myself in a strange, black abyss.
No noise could be heard, apart from my bare toes on the steel floor.
Suddenly – *crash!*
With footsteps as loud as thunder, I saw a storming purple blob-creature in the shape of a dragon.
I desperately felt around for a door or button, but all I could touch was air.
I ran out of time, the creature, storming near,
Its mouth was open, revealing a set of teeth as sharp as knives,
At the last second, I woke up, my body shaking violently,
The end of the dream.
But I still believe the darkness is lurking somewhere,
In the corner of the room.

But I'll just have to wait and see.

Evelyn O'Sullivan (9)
St Mary's Catholic Primary School, Madeley

What A Wonderful Dream

I had a dream
What a wonderful dream
I dreamt of Thor
And unicorns with horns.
I met the Satyr
And they deserted.
I met a Heffalump
Along with a Hufflepuff.
I talked to a Woozle
Who wasn't so rule-some.
I met a bat with a hat
Riding on a cat.
I relaxed with cats
Who wore hats and lay on their backs
I laid down with a rat on a mat.
I walked with mice
Who all had rice
I saw a tooth, fixing a hoof.
I talked to a tiger and a horse rider
I met a warrior who was an awful worrier
I opened my eyes and to my surprise
It was all a wonderful dream.

Laura Jane Lewis (9)
St Mary's Catholic Primary School, Madeley

Space And The Stars

S tanding on my little star
P eering out very far
A nd what I could see?
C ouldn't be good, because of me
E arth was there spinning around when the moon fell asleep

A nd crashed far down into the deep
N ow it hit the Earth with one big bang
D own went the Earth because one girl sang

S aturn was in trouble, what could they do?
T hen a star tried to stop it but went down too
A nd after that, the world went quiet so
R eally do not sing to a...
S tar or you'll cause a solar riot!

Ami-Lee Mary Roseblade (9)
St Mary's Catholic Primary School, Madeley

The Castle

A thick blanket of snow surrounded it,
Shooting stars flew around in a fit,
People started to wonder what the castle was all
about,
Was it haunted? Was it magical? Or even just a house?

Trees stood proud like 100 soldiers,
And bushes slouched down like a few old, grey
boulders,
Something seemed to entice you forward,
From your house and through the woods,
The castle had points that are knives,
It could kill someone with ten lives.

Doors as big as a giant,
And that is not even lying,
The castle reached to the sky,
Yes, it was really high!

Olivia Holt (11)
St Mary's Catholic Primary School, Madeley

The Magical Sea

The ocean is my destiny
But what is in this powerful sea?
Swim across it, do I dare?
This powerful thing gives me a scare
Could this be my only chance?
Should I give this thing a glance?
This mysterious light calls to me
As I follow it across the sea
I reach for the light and it draws me closer
I feel its power as it takes over
Soon enough its work is done
I'm now a mermaid having fun
Swimming in the deep blue sea,
With the fish and coral surrounding me
What great adventure awakens me now?
And will I return to land somehow?

Peyton Farmer (9)
St Mary's Catholic Primary School, Madeley

The Frog That Wanted To Fly

There was a frog at the pond,
I'm very blonde,
The frog saw a fly,
The fly was very high in the sky,
He wanted to leap,
But there was a big beak,
He wanted to leap on the beak,
But it was too high,
He had to lie,
He had to jump,
The bird trumped,
He said, "I'm flying,
I'm soaring in the sky!
I'm so high!"
I was sitting on the bird
I was about to hurl
I went over the clouds
It was peaceful
It was the end
I had a journey
I don't tell anyone, *shhh*.

Poppy Lowndes (7)
St Mary's Catholic Primary School, Madeley

A Magical Forest

A mazing sights everywhere.

M agic runs wild
A stonishing creatures hiding about
G oblins cackling with glee
I mps brewing up a plan
C aring, loving unicorns
A bandoned caves owned by dragons
L eprechauns guarding their pot of gold.

F airies dancing everywhere
O rcs feasting in the moonlight
R aging beasts coming out to play
E nchanted pixies casting spells
S oaring griffins in the sky
T his forest is wonderous!

Amy Thomas (9)
St Mary's Catholic Primary School, Madeley

My Worst Nightmare

One dark, gloomy night
I was in a tremendous fight
I was very sneaky
The pipe was a bit leaky.

I snuck into a haunted museum
I had a lot of enthusiasm
I saw vampire's fangs
And there were also some bands.

The books were floating
The witches were gloating
I got sucked into a book
I had a very close look
I got very lost
It had a big cost.

I saw a big giant
And it was defiant
I found my way out
And I was dancing about.

Bindiya Aujla (8)
St Mary's Catholic Primary School, Madeley

Dragon Cove

D own in the dungeon-like cave
R aging dragons hide in passageways
A dimly glowing crimson light
G argling noises cause lots of fright.
O nly two adventurers may survive
N o one knows the deceased explorer I can't revive

C astles damage and set on fire the ground
O ver the destruction, a dragon cub is lost and now is found
V ersions of my mind said they were friendly
E liott and I decided to befriend it!

Bethany Thomas (10)
St Mary's Catholic Primary School, Madeley

The Dancing Ostrich

There's this wonderful creature,
That runs really fast,
Which has a weird feature,
That you can't run past

She can twirl and flip,
Run and prance,
It's a marvellous trick,
She can dance!

From ballet to hip hop,
Which takes your breath away,
She shall never stop,
Good stuff people say

There's this wonderful creature,
That runs really fast,
Which has a weird feature,
That you can't run past.

Fearne Scarlett Rose Finnigan (10)
St Mary's Catholic Primary School, Madeley

Cat City

My dream led me in a strange place, with cats around me
How did it get there?
The cats looked too soft to touch, I got up and took a step forward
The cats stared at me, their eyes were glowing like party lights
When I kept taking steps forward they kept following me
I realised I was in the cat city
That's why there were cats all around, staring at me
With their glowing eyes, I found out I woke up in my bed
And forgot it was all just a dream.

River Ann Jones (9)
St Mary's Catholic Primary School, Madeley

Lost

I was lost in the woods
Nowhere to be found
It was dark and cold
And wet on the ground.

It was very windy
Very, very cold
I looked for a branch
To hug and hold.

'Cause I was so wet
And so cold
"I need to get up," I said to myself
"I need to escape
From this bad fairy tale."

And so I did
I opened my eyes
I was in my room
Admiring the blue sky.

Fabian Ciornei (10)
St Mary's Catholic Primary School, Madeley

Bulldogs

B ulldogs are awesome
R otten, they're not
I nsects they chase
T iny tails
I rritated by the sun
S tinky pumps
H appy all the time.

B ounce all day
U gly? Definitely not
L ively when you meet them
L ittle and large
D aydream all the time
O verly stupid
G orgeous
S lobber everywhere.

Amelia Rose Havard (8)
St Mary's Catholic Primary School, Madeley

A Mystical World

Once I had a statue
That looked like a fairy and her name was Jemima
She suddenly came to life
Then I was teleported to Fairyland with Jemima
I felt free, joyful and wild
It looked like a forest because there were trees, a pond
Wands, magic mushrooms and other fairies
I jumped on the mushroom trampoline, got wind and
flew
But finally, I had to go home but managed to find
mythical areas.

Davina Mann (7)
St Mary's Catholic Primary School, Madeley

Fairy Garden

As I walk in the garden, I see a little house
It lights up and looks magical
I wonder who lives there, maybe a dormouse
As I look through the window
I can see a twinkle
There is a little path of tiny footprints
A tail of glistening dust leads the way
I look around the corner and see some wings glint
I think I know who lives there, can I say?
It's a secret fairy house.

Izabella Thomas (7)
St Mary's Catholic Primary School, Madeley

Clowns

I recognised the voices calling me.

After taking a look through the window
I saw something such as two clowns in the middle of
the clouds.

I opened the window and flew over to reach them but
they were so far,
I was scared and shaking, I was going to fall
I started crying and calling Mum for help.

At the same time, I felt a hand keeping me up
It was my friend.

Luca Eitel Fotso (8)
St Mary's Catholic Primary School, Madeley

The Best Dream In The World!

My dream this night was a very special one
I found a unicorn eating...
Some delicious, delicious corn
In the moonlight
Dancing till his feet came off
He ran in a fright
He came and said to me,
"Who are you?"
"I'm Lee, can I be your friend?"
"Yes!"
And we went off
When we got into Lee's bedroom
The unicorn was a teddy!

Wilma-Thelma Sam (9)
St Mary's Catholic Primary School, Madeley

Hero

I'm a superhero
I fly around the town
I love being a hero
I have to wear a beautiful gown
I find and fight the villain
I fly up in the clouds
There's no time for chillin'
As the villain is flying around
I must stop him now
Before he defeats the town
I punch and kick him so he's down
And banish him from showing his face in the town.

Taylor-May Skyvington (8)
St Mary's Catholic Primary School, Madeley

Lost

I went for a walk one day
And much to my dismay
I got lost, not completely lost
But I couldn't find my way
I looked left, I looked right
But there was nothing in my sight
I walked in towards the dark
I was never the brightest spark!
Nothing was certain, so I looked behind the curtain
Completely lost but I couldn't find my way!

Zsa-Zsa Rowland (8)
St Mary's Catholic Primary School, Madeley

Magical Adventure

U p we go into the sky
N evermind, I can fly
I can see the most beautiful things
C olours all around and same massive wings
O n a magical adventure, we will go
R ainbows and clouds, it's all going so slow
N ever have I seen a land made of sweets
S uch an amazing night filled with treats.

Kacy-Leigh Kniveton (7)

St Mary's Catholic Primary School, Madeley

These Yummy Biscuits

B iscuits are very tasty
I 'm so happy with all the biscuits
S weet like all the Jammie Dodgers
C runchy like all the ginger biscuits
U nhateable like a vanilla icing cake
I 'm so full up of my yummy biscuits
T oo much sweetness for all my friends
S ugary like some Sugar Puffs.

Ethan Humphries (8)
St Mary's Catholic Primary School, Madeley

Dancing Is Destiny

D estiny is to follow your heart

A nd no one can tell you how to do it

N ow I have a passion and that's to dance

C urling and twirling, that's what I do

I n life, you do what you think is right

N ow, I am no expert at dancing

G o and have a go, you never know. It could be your destiny.

Teigan Skyvington (10)
St Mary's Catholic Primary School, Madeley

Fluffy Clouds

When I was on the cloud, I felt something fluffy
I looked down and I saw... a cloud
And you know it was very fluffy
It wasn't very, very, very, very loud
I saw a very beautiful rainbow
But it didn't rain though
I felt very happy!
Even though I felt quite flappy
Yes, I was with my mom
And her name was not Tom.

Elisha Pledger (7)
St Mary's Catholic Primary School, Madeley

Dragon City

Last night, I dreamt about Dragon City
I was in the game
I couldn't stop playing
Hundred and hundreds of dragons
They were in McDonald's
They are not only beasts
They are friends
With long tails and golden eyes
They can dance
And we have a chance
To play a game
And get fun the same.

Vladut Cristian Popa (8)
St Mary's Catholic Primary School, Madeley

A Miracle

S tarfish was what I met

T winkles went through their eyes

A villain was what I met

R oughly, I was brave enough to stay

F ish around were swimming

I barely noticed I had powers

S un was what I saw in the darkness

H ooray! Everyone cheered. I became a hero.

Jessica Griffiths (7)
St Mary's Catholic Primary School, Madeley

Dragon Dreams

D ragons are mythical beasts that fly
R ight to left, they soar through the sky
A bove the clouds, they tend to survive
G reat troves of treasure they tend to hide
O ver mountains, they will glide
N o human may be seen again
S o don't be seen near their den.

Jordan Van Jaarsveld (10)
St Mary's Catholic Primary School, Madeley

Summer

I went to the sea
My friend was funny
My mum loves me
The weather is sunny
It was such a good day
We all gave a cheer
I saw a tree
I very much hear
Girls call boys, *he*
We all went to the beach
I like to go to the shop
I also teach
I wear my favourite top.

Meghan Canty (8)
St Mary's Catholic Primary School, Madeley

Miss Foxy

M y teacher is a fox
I can't wait to see
S he can only see in black and white
S he has orange hair.

F oxes might look scary but they are not
O h, how I love Miss Foxy
X -rays of foxes she shows us
Y ou might be a fox!

Zuzanna Milczarek (10)
St Mary's Catholic Primary School, Madeley

A Fairy's Tale

F airy, fairy, in my dream
A nd everything is so clean
I 'm sure I saw a fairy, yes!
R osy was her name, but she wanted me to guess
I would really like Rosy to stay
E specially as she likes to play
S adly, she flew away.

Imogen Groom (8)
St Mary's Catholic Primary School, Madeley

Spider, Spider

One little day
One little man
One little dream
One little scream.

Because he knew
The sky was not blue
Spiders came down, crowned
Like they owned a tool
They took over his land
They took his hand
And the crown was theirs.

Joshua Hughes (8)
St Mary's Catholic Primary School, Madeley

Dragon

Strongest dragon, rise his wings
Now he sees many things
Flying loudly in the sky
Looking scary in the sky
Flames of fire scare us all
What should we do at all?
Run or hide or scream, help!
The dragon will destroy us all.

Benos Juskevicius (8)
St Mary's Catholic Primary School, Madeley

The School

There was a little school
As always, we are learning there
Sitting, I heard, *crash. Bang. Boom.*
Then the school breaks down
A little confused, we all look outside
Then we were in a forest.

Lena Sulkowska (9)
St Mary's Catholic Primary School, Madeley

Football Mania!

I liked to play football in the hall
Or sometimes I just kick it against the wall
And one time I kicked it so far and tall
And when I score a goal
The crowd screamed and roared.

Isabelle Maddison White (8)
St Mary's Catholic Primary School, Madeley

Athlete

Last night when I was fast asleep
I dreamt I was an awesome athlete
I heard the crowd cheer my name
The blast of the gun set me off.

Last night when I was fast asleep
I dreamt I was an amazing athlete
I saw vicious, flashing lights
The dazzling, mighty medals were now in sight.

Last night when I was fast asleep
I dreamt I was an astonishing athlete
I trained and trained till it hurt my brain
But my legs were ready to win the game.

Last night when I was fast asleep
I woke up and realised I can be an athlete
I need to train hard and set my goals high
And maybe one day that medal will be mine.

Joshua George Walton (9)
St Matthew's CE (A) Primary School, Donnington

The Discovery Of The Dinosaur

In the night sky, the stars come into sight
Where will my dreams take me tonight?
I can't believe what I saw
Are they really footprints of a dinosaur?

I see light shining on a waterfall far away
I hear a mysterious noise, should I stay?
I move a branch so that I can see
There is something lying against the tree.

I try to get closer to explore
Wow! It's a big fat dinosaur
He's purple and has three horns on his head
And is using the jungle floor as his bed.

Closer and closer I quietly creep
Please, please dinosaur, stay asleep
But suddenly I see an eye on me
Shall I stay or shall I flee?

I stand still and give a friendly smile
My feet ready to run a mile
The dinosaur moves and stands at a great height
He really is a magnificent sight.

There really wasn't much to fear
As the dinosaur smiled at me from ear to ear
He bent his long neck and I climbed on his back
Now we are running down a rocky track.

Stomping through fields of beautiful flowers
We played together for hours and hours
Splashing in the waterfall pool
"Wake up, sleepy, it's time for school."

Lilly Hovers (8)
St Modwen's Catholic Primary School, Burton-On-Trent

A Dream Full Of Wonder

I wondered...
I wondered who makes our dreams
I wondered what everything we dream about means.

I wondered if there were any worlds beyond the largest hill, so I travelled until...

I discovered a wondercloud where tiny crystals and sparkly dust danced around.

I discovered a wonderground, where happy children and funny creatures played together, safe and sound.

I discovered a wonderstar that magically transformed into a flying car.

Together we travelled far and far
We travelled to the unknown, we travelled where no human could go.

We travelled till dawn, and then the magic star was gone.

I opened my eyes just to see how wonderful my dreams can be.

Now, I wonder what the future will bring
When I grow up and leave my parents' wings?

I wonder what my future will show
Which direction my dreams will flow?

I wonder...

Maksymilian Zimnoch (10)
St Modwen's Catholic Primary School, Burton-On-Trent

The Land Of Dreams

Every night I dream of it
The land where anything is possible
The land where you dream it and it comes to life
The land of dreams.

The time my dreams came to life
The amazing land full of dreams
I entered and
Whoosh! Whish!
It was the sound of all the boys and girls coming to life
The cotton candy trees as fluffy as beautiful soft clouds
The fairies and elves dancing in joy
The sun looking down at me
I was amazed!

But soon the happiness faded
The sky went dark and gloomy
The dreams were being lost
The feeling that my dreams will turn into a nightmare.

I knew something was wrong
The joy of the land was dying
The sky started to cry
All the fun and joy go
Just as that happened

There was a cheering voice
It was enough to get the happiness back
But something was definitely still wrong.

Jayami Dinara Hewawasan Ranaweerage (9)
St Modwen's Catholic Primary School, Burton-On-Trent

All About Ballerinas

Ballerinas are like dancing swans in the air
Nearly every ballerina imagines that they have pure
white
Outstanding wings that can fly across the stage
And amaze people with a massive, "Wow!"

Although ballerinas have one special power
Here in this world must be one ballerina
Which has two very special powers
And knows the future of her life in front of her face.

This amazing ballerina had beautiful gold, long hair
And dances like a weightless feather floating in the air
And slowly getting itself down
She had a baby pink tutu and a baby purple crop top
She loved dancing and knew that when she grew up
She would perform with the world's best ballerinas
And her dreams always come true in the end
She was only twelve but she had her whole life in front
of her.

Nikola Zuralska (10)
St Modwen's Catholic Primary School, Burton-On-Trent

Earth Fairy

I was walking to the bus stop. The sun was shining, the birds were singing, and everyone was happy. Until the sky darkened and lightning struck down and shook the Earth with all its strength. I hid behind the barrel as I heard footsteps, like someone wanted to capture me. I thought that I was wrong but instead I was right. They made a circle and tried to send me somewhere but a bit of magic pulled me out. I didn't know where it came from. Until I noticed it was from fairies. I totally freaked out. They told me to believe in fairies. As I believed in fairies, their power became more powerful until they got new powers. After five minutes, the fairies won the battle. Then I transformed into a fairy, and from that day on, I was always by the fairies side, and we always fight crimes and we lived happily ever after.

Leya Jacob (7)
St Modwen's Catholic Primary School, Burton-On-Trent

Galaxy Of The Unicorns

On a dark and starry night, just the other day
I looked up to the sky beyond the Milky Way
Was a galaxy shining right before my eyes
It was exciting, colourful and I realised
There was a star with an open door
So I stepped inside onto a sparkling floor.

The clouds were candyfloss, the floor was pink
It was amazing, brilliant, I couldn't blink
But then I saw the most amazing thing ever -
Glistening and sparkling through the chocolate rainy
weather
Was a horn
The size of my Dad's phone
Like an upside-down ice cream cone
I looked closer and closer, my heart skipped a beat
I saw unicorns play and dance at my feet.

Suddenly, I jumped, I woke up with a blink
Looked out of my window - there was a unicorn that
winked!

Daniella Hathaway (10)
St Modwen's Catholic Primary School, Burton-On-Trent

Nightmare Hell!

Walking around the strawberry lake
Worn and frightened look on your face
Volcano of death could anytime erupt
Death King, your tour guide, vicious and abrupt.

Evil supervillains line the lake
You're thinking about the escape you could make
Clutching your friend with all your might
Scared and upset, you want to take flight.

When all of a sudden, a terrifying bang
You jump with a start and can see a large gang
You rub your eyes to see much clearer
As they approach and get nearer and nearer.

It's not those evil supervillains you see
But my mum who's shaking and waking me
Thank goodness it was all a bad dream
There's no evil Death King, there would seem.

Oscar Lomas (9)
St Modwen's Catholic Primary School, Burton-On-Trent

Swan Lake

As the sky changes into night
I imagine the moon as my spotlight
I close my eyes for my dream that awaits
My dancing future I create.

As I stand in the middle of the stage
I can feel my heart against my ribcage
One last look that my ribbons are tight
Final deep breath, no time for stage fright.

As the music begins, I feel all eyes on me
Just need to remember the steps one, two and three
The feathers connecting my dress swooshing in time
Light catching the jewels, making them shine.

As I glide and float around the stage floor
I always want to dance some more
Returning to the centre, hoping for an applause
But it's now time to put this dream on pause.

Megan Hovers (10)
St Modwen's Catholic Primary School, Burton-On-Trent

My Fairyland Dream

Last night I had the best dream ever
As I lay down in my bed
I climbed over a magnificent rainbow
And magic filled my head
I visited the wonderful Fairyland
Full of magic, dust and doors
I crept around so quietly
And completed the Fairyland tours
The magical land was full of toadstools
Red and white and round
I skipped and danced around them
But was careful not to make a sound
The fairies were all asleep you see
In their tiny, fairy beds
They looked extremely comfortable
As they rested their tiny fairy heads
I loved my visit to Fairyland
I will always remember it well
The only problem is that I have to try
To keep it a secret and not to tell.

Ava Mae Cruise (8)
St Modwen's Catholic Primary School, Burton-On-Trent

No Voice ~ My Nightmare

I wake up and look for my sister
She's not there
I shout for my parents
I can't hear my voice.

It feels like my heartbeat's in my head
Bouncing back and forth off my eardrum
I still can't hear my voice

I shout as loud as I can
But I only hear the echoes in my ear
I can't hear my voice!

I can't hear me
Can anyone else?
I still have no voice.

My breathing is heavy and I'm losing focus
I panic
I have no voice.

I hear footsteps in my room
I turn to look and I see
The person that I need to be right next to me...

My mum, she had heard my voice call out to her.

Edward Fletcher-McCraight (10)
St Modwen's Catholic Primary School, Burton-On-Trent

My House Is Amazing

My house is amazing
It's made out of Pikachus
It is tall, pink and beautiful
Then I go inside
It looks like a rainbow
With fluffy cotton all over the place
And every Pokémon you could imagine
As well as, Croagunk, Pikachu, Cottonee, Turtwig
And Toxicroak, there were much, much, more.

My house is amazing
It's got a gigantic garden
With Pokémon playing with me
Also, it has a pool, which Greninja likes
My house also has a 3DS
I could play with my Pokémon every day
I could also watch a whole of cartoons
With my Pokémon, I could ride on a shell
My house is amazing.

Connie Costelloe (9)
St Modwen's Catholic Primary School, Burton-On-Trent

The Final Fight!

Hello, old friend, it's nice to see you
I just really don't want to beat you
I guess this is it, we will fight
Me and you both know this won't end bright.

Don't you realise, it's me your friend?
Please don't make this the end
Please stop, you're making me cry
And I really don't want to die.

We have had so many good memories together
This will not make anything better
Old friend, why are you killing me?
Now I am dead, you will never see me.

Oh no! I have killed my friend
This will be his end
Don't worry, I will make it up to you
I guess I will join him too.

Ben Jacob (10)
St Modwen's Catholic Primary School, Burton-On-Trent

Lost In Space

L osing control in the endless void
O ur spaceship's been struck by an asteroid
S uddenly, it feels like there's no way back
T umbling, turning through the inky black

I 've come face to face with the worst of my fears
N o! If I give in it will only bring tears.

S pace rocks swirling all around
P lanets watch without making a sound
A paint-splattered canvas hangs over my head
C ontact's been lost - my last hope is dead
E xhale - relief! I've just woken up in bed...

Samuel Benstead (9)
St Modwen's Catholic Primary School, Burton-On-Trent

Mondane Town

Silently, I entered
To see what awaits
I'm not going to wait for fate
Creeping inside
I feel a shiver down my spine.

I look up and see
A sign that wanted me to flee:
Mondane Town
Nightmares Abound,
Watch Your Back
You Can't Relax!

It happened so fast
It sounded like a snap
So I turned on my heels
And something felt...
Sort of...
Strange...

They were staring at me
There were two or three
Ghosts!

But then I realised
To my despise
A horde was right behind me!

Alexis Mabatid (10)
St Modwen's Catholic Primary School, Burton-On-Trent

The Unicorn In My Room

I was in my bed
Hugging my teddy called Ted
Suddenly, it all turned bright
Like the moon in the middle of the night.

I looked around my house
But all I could see was a lighthouse
When suddenly I saw more light
But it was sparkling white.

It was the unicorn of my dreams
But it was way better than it seemed
Hair as colourful as a rainbow
Skin as white as snow.

A second later, the unicorn was gone
But it left a picture of a swan
I never told anyone about this night
Because it won't be quite right.

Anna James (10)
St Modwen's Catholic Primary School, Burton-On-Trent

Dream Land

As I drift off to sleep
Every night, I take a peep
Of a land I found
Dream Land!

A magical place
Covered in strawberry lace
An oozing chocolate fountain
Dribbling milkshake down the mountain!

Enchanting animals everywhere
Alpacas and reindeer here and there
Sweet birds chirp to wake you
To watch the sunrise, a ball of treats rise from Lake
Milkshake.

But best of all, I love the fact
That a bundle of everything you love packed
And anything is possible
Nothing ever happens that is horrible.

Annmiya Tharappel (10)
St Modwen's Catholic Primary School, Burton-On-Trent

The Battle Of The Dancing Unicorn

Here comes the unicorn
Dancing the beat of her favourite song
She slides and she glides
She kicks and dives.

Here comes trouble, make it double
The dance comes swirling and twirling
Jumping and flying, repeating her master.

Bashing into each other comes a disaster
Battle, here we come, get out the drums
A ballet of beauty begins as the two commence battle.

Louder and louder the music gets, makes an
earthquake inside your head
The unicorn's hair waves whilst the dancer's tutu spins
like Dad.

Jerusha James (9)
St Modwen's Catholic Primary School, Burton-On-Trent

Flower Tower Tree

I suddenly wake up
In a beautiful world
I see lots of flowers
On the castle's top.

It's pastel pink
And then I think
Could this be true?
I had no clue.

There are trees covered in sweet, gummy bears
And next to them are unbreakable chairs
But the main thing I could see
Was the flower tower tree.

It has multicoloured flowers
And it is as big as the Eiffel Tower
All over it, there is cream
But then I realised it was just a dream.

Michalina Dytrych (10)
St Modwen's Catholic Primary School, Burton-On-Trent

A Life In Paradise Full Of Mystery

Life in paradise, paradise all around my lifetime.
No wonder it's such a wonderful island, with peaceful silence.
I found a fast, strong river, it gave me the shivers,
It freezes my feet, so I take a big leap.
I teleported to every galaxy, like a vision of mystery.
I was amazed so much, I had such luck.
I had such freedom, I could never have such boredom.
I saw a running star, I followed it, then I travelled to Mars.

Then I heard silence...

Benjamin Aaron Paredes Amigo (9)
St Modwen's Catholic Primary School, Burton-On-Trent

Dreaming

D arting forward to whatever holds within

R esting in bed all comfy and tight

E xtraordinary sights to see and believe

A crazy adventure set beyond possibility

M agical and phenomenal, as great as can be

I magination - a large wide box as far as the eye can see

N ew and extreme stories ahead in the wonderful world of imagination

G reat and exciting stories are to be told, so let's see as they unfold.

Marc Antony Howells (10)

St Modwen's Catholic Primary School, Burton-On-Trent

Bad Hair Day

I look in the mirror
In shock and despair
What's wrong with my hair?
It's just not fair.

It's as brown as chocolate and very wavy
Everyone looks at me like I'm crazy
It sways along on my back
You could even mistake it for a cat.

It smells of flowers when I wash and dry it
I even use a comb to try and style it.

But I'm not using some silly, smelly hairspray
It's just another bad hair day.

Elena Charalambous (10)
St Modwen's Catholic Primary School, Burton-On-Trent

The Night Of Doom

I don't know where I should be
But all I see is someone staring right at me.

A blast and a boom are all I hear
But then I hear that sound of doom coming near.

When I run I hear a sound and
All I know is that it is coming from the ground.

I really hope that someone's coming
But suddenly I hear a person humming.

I run to the exit but then I realised,
That's it or *otherwise!*

Daniel Kolodziej (9)
St Modwen's Catholic Primary School, Burton-On-Trent

The Moon

Hello, Moon
I love to see you every night
Your sparkling light and shine
I like you when you are big and round
As well as you are small with a smiley face.

I wonder where you are today?
Are you hiding from me or
Are the clouds hiding you from me?
Are you shy to come out?

Whatever the reason
Please come out
I can't sleep without your smiley face looking at me
I'm waiting for you.

Leon Jacob
St Modwen's Catholic Primary School, Burton-On-Trent

The Gorgeous Garden

In my beautiful garden,
There hides one secret, perfect plant
Nothing ever goes on its leaf,
Not even an ant.

Its flower is as red as a rose
And in the night it brightly glows
It attracts insects, big and small
It attracts me, you and all.

My friendly flower never fails
Not even when its face pales
It's now time to say that...

My flower is a red, foolish tulip!

Abel Tharappel (7)
St Modwen's Catholic Primary School, Burton-On-Trent

Darkside

D arkish nightmare begins right now

A fter running away, the lights glow

R epent from happy things, this is the Darkside

K ingdom of Darkside, Brightside stays behind

S lithering ghosts? Is this a joke?

I nside out, then something spoke

D eciding deeply, get me to the sunset-coloured dreams

E verything you do, everything the ghost sees.

Agata Maria Ignatiuk (9)
St Modwen's Catholic Primary School, Burton-On-Trent

Butterflies

B eautiful things flying in my garden
U nder the nice blue sky
T rying to do a dance
T ap dance, ballet, waltz
E veryone admires them
R ound and round
F lying up high and right down
L iving the life to fullest
I n my garden under the sun
E very hot summer day
S pread your wings and fly.

Ania Maria Kunicka (10)
St Modwen's Catholic Primary School, Burton-On-Trent

Nature Is Everywhere

Nature is everywhere
Everywhere you go.

Nature is everything
Everything that lives and grows.

Animals, plants and trees
They grow big and small
Tall and tiny.

In every way, nature is beautiful
Exciting and wonderful
And needs gentle care.

Please do your part
Help and protect
To keep nature forever beautiful.

Isaac Kiley (9)
St Modwen's Catholic Primary School, Burton-On-Trent

The Dream Wonderland

An island beneath a sunny sky
Lingering onward dreamily
On the evening of July.

It started on a Monday
You think that's bad?
Listen to this and you'll be glad.

This is your dream world
It is not like you heard
This is your Wonderland

Family and friends in one place
The sweet family homes
In the dream Wonderland.

Gaspar Zajdlewicz (10)
St Modwen's Catholic Primary School, Burton-On-Trent

Superpowers

I am walking around, I fall over on a rock
And my hands start electrocuting
Wow! I've got superpowers!

They are insane, I can electrify stuff
I have super speed
If anyone needs help,
I'll run straight to them
And help with my powers, superpowers.

Even though it was a dream
It's good
Once upon a dream.

Dillon Moore (10)
St Modwen's Catholic Primary School, Burton-On-Trent

Our Space

Our Solar System is
Like a family circling
Its own mother.

Our galaxy is like milk
Being spilt to make a spiral.

Jupiter is like hot chocolate
Poured and a red, spotted tomato.

Uranus is like blue water mixed with
Milk to make its colour.

Venus is like a gassed rock with
Brown odour.

Monika Olechowska (9)
St Modwen's Catholic Primary School, Burton-On-Trent

Trip

In my dream, I saw a car
I set off but didn't go far
I got out of the car and went in the bar
"Hello, is anyone here? I come from not far."
No one said anything, so I said, "I will go to the car."
I ran out of fuel
And thought, *that's not cool*
I went to bed
And that's all I said.

Martyna Anna Denis (10)
St Modwen's Catholic Primary School, Burton-On-Trent

The Dream

I wake up
To only see my end
In the hands of the pigman
To my surprise, he is strangling me.

I see the light
I try to grab it but
I felt the slimy texture of its nose.

But in my hand
I feel a metal, hand sword
I take the sword and raise it
Suddenly, everything is bright
I'm awake.

Seb H (10)
St Modwen's Catholic Primary School, Burton-On-Trent

The Runaway Butterfly

If you ever meet a butterfly, you would expect them to not talk
If you ever meet a butterfly, it won't look like a hawk
If you ever meet a butterfly, it would fly, of course
If you ever meet a butterfly, you would like it to fly
And actually, it would fly in PE pumps
My butterfly is black and white to give you a fright.

Libby Clarke (8)
St Modwen's Catholic Primary School, Burton-On-Trent

Mythically

O, unicorn with coat so dark
Your beauty is perfectly divine
With all my heart and soul
I wish you were real.

For if you were, I'd love you so
And protect you from all the harm
So all the world come to know you're real
The magic of your charm.

Angelina Sebastian (9)
St Modwen's Catholic Primary School, Burton-On-Trent

Unicorns

U seful animal comes in handy

N ever naughty!

I ncredible at being friends

C an smell people suffering from miles away

O f course, they need to be fed rainbow food

R eally kind

N ever evil

S uper amazing!

Blanka Zajdlewicz (8)
St Modwen's Catholic Primary School, Burton-On-Trent

Dinosaur

D inosaur there, dinosaur everywhere

I ndescribable killer

N ew reign of dinosaurs

O utrageous beast

S cary stomp, loud, terrifying!

A new terror

U ntameable monster

R oar, roar, roar!

Jared Pestano (10)

St Modwen's Catholic Primary School, Burton-On-Trent

Oliver

O liver is cool and amazing
L ittle bit cheeky
I 'm a musician
V ery calm
E xtraordinary boy
R eally smart.

Oliver Senior (9)
St Modwen's Catholic Primary School, Burton-On-Trent

Witch Catastrophe

One dark, dark night,
I see a bright light,
The Olympics are on,
And I am gone.

Wait... a witch, how?
What? Is it Halloween now?
It might be my imagination,
What is that creation?

In the distance, I see a white cat,
Sitting... are they sat on a bat?
What is happening? What are they doing?
"Run away now," I say, shooing.

Oh no! The witch is coming towards me.
What should I do now? Is that an exit I see?
I run and I run and I run some more,
And finally made it through the door.

Home at last, safe and sound,
Not a chance I will be found,
I slowly begin to open my eyes,
And pretty soon I realise...

It was all a dream.

Summer Ratcliffe (9)
Stoke Minster CE Primary Academy, Stoke-On-Trent

Ariana Grande

A mazing as can be, she is my star
R ight now I dream to be a singer like her
I am always excited when she is on the radio
A riana is the top number one!
N ow I am always excited when she is on the radio
A riana, never give up when you know you're a star

G ive your fans what they deserve, keep dreaming
R elate to the radio because you never give up
A lways be my star and for evermore
N ever give up
D on't let anything let you down
E veryone is counting on you to be the best singer.

Olivia Grace Steele (10)

Stoke Minster CE Primary Academy, Stoke-On-Trent

Key To The Portal

One portal a time
One key to start
All portals are perfectly fine
Quicker than the fastest kart.

I have been lost for very long
Please keep calm, please stay strong
Use your powers with all your might
Everything will be alright.

Am I in London?
I've got to get to Stoke
I must get there soon
Hope I don't croak!

They were coming for me - trying to kill
Well... if I don't pay their bill
Frozen in fear, I stood so still
I will defend myself at will.

Ayaan Hussain (10)
Stoke Minster CE Primary Academy, Stoke-On-Trent

The Lost Boy

Round and round my head goes.
And I don't know where I am, but someone knows.

In a dream or not... I wonder.
Now the rains come, wait what's that? It's... It's a kitty.

Finally, I found it... It's a city!
Oh no! It's the forest and there's a kitty.

Right, I'll pick up the kitty and go to the woods
Did you hear that? I think it was thudding.

Sun in the city... I hear a scream
Time to wake up, it's only a dream.

Ryan Davies (10)
Stoke Minster CE Primary Academy, Stoke-On-Trent

Daring Danger Dimensions!

D reaming of the lands I see

I see the dimensions out at sea

M y wonderful crew goes and

E xplores in fields of planets, as I dive into a black hole like a gannet

N ever existing species now exist

S oaring through the air, I see the mists

I have my eyes glistening on the stars and

O n the way, I visit Mars

N everending planet coloured red

S uddenly, I wake up to find I'm safe in bed.

Abirsana Gnanavadivel (9)

Stoke Minster CE Primary Academy, Stoke-On-Trent

Young**Writers**

Once Upon A Dream

C heering fans awaiting

R oaring fans as soon as a catch comes by

I n the cricket match, I hit the ball so hard, it soars up into the sky

C ricketers jumping and cheering

K nowingly, the bowler strikes for the wickets

E agerly waiting for the fielders - wait for a catch

T he last ball comes and it's whacked into the air.

Ali Shah (10)

Stoke Minster CE Primary Academy, Stoke-On-Trent

Into The Black Hole

As I flew into space I saw a black hole
I was in my rocket as it started to roll.

As I come to a stop
I feel terrified
I can see a digital dimension on one side.

A dangerous dragon is getting near
I see my digital chest armour appear
I take out my shield and sword
And the dragon is no more
I wake up and it's all a dream.

Cody Stone (10)
Stoke Minster CE Primary Academy, Stoke-On-Trent

Dream Dancer

In my dream, I am in a dance studio
In my dream, I am with my best friends
In my dream, I can see mirrors as huge as skyscrapers
In my dream, I learn to dance on a superstar stage
In my dream, my friends and I are really excited
In my dream, my friends win the competition
In my dream, we win a golden trophy with number one written on it.

Agata Maslowska (10)
Stoke Minster CE Primary Academy, Stoke-On-Trent

Fossil Hunter

Once upon a dream, I became a fossil hunter
Once upon a dream, I excavated a stegosaurus skeleton
Once upon a dream, I found the femur of an allosaurus
Once upon a dream, the prehistoric dinosaur bones
Have been taken by a museum
Once upon a dream, They have been on display
Once upon a dream, it all started again but with other bones.

Martin Bevilagua (10)
Stoke Minster CE Primary Academy, Stoke-On-Trent

Cool Comics

C ome around, listen to my comics
O ne day my characters came to life
M aybe soon you will be worthy
I n the night, I fight crime, maybe you will sometimes
C an you hear the superhero calls?
S winging around the neighbourhood like a monkey.

Logan Adams (10)
Stoke Minster CE Primary Academy, Stoke-On-Trent

Mountains Of Ice Cream

I have a dream about ice cream,
With monstrous cherries on top.
It cleans my mouth with yumminess...
Just like a mop.
I'm standing on a wafer cone,
Overlooking a huge chocolate flake alone.
Mountains of ice cream,
I dream, I dream, I dream.

Noor Mohammed (10)
Stoke Minster CE Primary Academy, Stoke-On-Trent

Dancing Queen

F amous dance in the sky,
A s I dream, I dream I cannot fly,
M y life as a dancer, steady as can be,
O ut in a limo, who's in charge...? Me!
U nder security, no fuss,
S o much money, such a rush!

Libby Mae Smith (10)
Stoke Minster CE Primary Academy, Stoke-On-Trent

Ghosts...

G hosts are scary

H alloween's their night

O minous phantoms

S inister spirits

T hey're under your bed and in your closet

S o go to sleep and they won't bite!

Haseeb Hussain (10)
Stoke Minster CE Primary Academy, Stoke-On-Trent

Daydreams

The sky is the best,
When you imagine...
Fluffy clouds like rays,
Going so fast.
Then you close your eyes,
And quickly open them again,
And *boom!*... a year has gone!

Fatima Tariq Rughiem (10)
Stoke Minster CE Primary Academy, Stoke-On-Trent

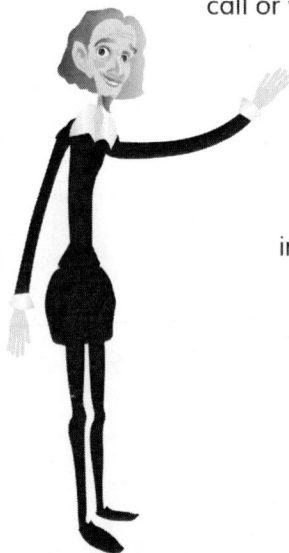